Whippoorwill Farewell

Jocassee Remembered

by

Debbie Fletcher

"Close your eyes, and read it with your heart."

Trafford rev. 03/13/2019

 www.trafford.com

North America & international
toll-free: 1 888 232 4444 (USA & Canada)
fax: 812 355 4082

This book may not be politically correct;

In some instances, it may not be grammatically correct.

But the memories are thick and deserving of a much better epitaph

Than forever being laid to rest at the bottom of deep water . . .

If only for my children.

~ Debbie Fletcher

In loving memory of Mother
Betty Lutrelle Williams Richardson

About 8 years ago, I started writing my memories of Jocassee for my girls to read one day. A few months later, I had the privilege of meeting Dot Jackson, a gifted author, who sat at the kitchen table reading my story and told me through her tears, "You have to publish this." In my wildest imagination, I never dreamed that would be possible, but Dot persisted in reminding me from time to time that I'd "better be writing that book!" So, Dot . . . this book is dedicated to you.

My husband Dave has supported me 110% in this entire project. I don't know how many nights he would come upstairs late at night while I worked at the computer and ask if I was ever coming to bed. He has patiently tolerated more Jocassee stories than any "northern boy" should ever have to hear. So, honey . . . this book is also dedicated to you.

My girls, Melissa and Pam, and my precious granddaughters, Miranda and Olivia, are my heartbeat. Girls . . . this book is also dedicated to you.

My Jocassee memories are all wrapped up in family, especially my mother Betty and brother Jimmy. This book is also dedicated to you.

To my heroes, Bill Routh, Charles Johnson, and Jackie Smith. Bill, since your first phone call to me a year and a half ago, you have not only dedicated your time and resources to finding Attakulla Lodge, but you have been there to encourage me when I heard continual rumors that the Lodge had floated off her foundation. Finding the Lodge intact would never have been possible without you. So, Bill . . . this book is also dedicated to you.

Jackie and Charles , you have literally put your life at risk to dive to a depth of 300 feet to confirm first-hand that Attakulla Lodge is indeed still standing. Your enthusiasm and support has meant the world to me, and the amazing gift you retrieved for me – the sidelight that used to stand beside the front door – is a rare treasure. One of my biggest regrets for the past 33 years has been that we never thought to take some token of remembrance from the Lodge – even just a door knob or a spindle from the bannister. My favorite Bible verse is Psalm 37:4: "Delight yourself in the Lord, and He will give you the desires of your heart." God used you that day to give me a desire of my heart. Charles and Jackie . . . this book is also dedicated to you.

Table of Contents

Foreword

Jocassee Valley, peacefully tucked in the arms of the Blue Ridge Mountains in Oconee County, was finally laid to rest in 1973. Duke Power Company's multi-million dollar Keowee-Toxaway hydroelectric dam project abruptly choked the natural flow of four wild rivers: Whitewater, Toxaway, Horsepasture and Keowee, inundating the Valley under a chilling shroud, in some places over 300 feet deep. The idyllic sights and sounds of Jocassee are forever lost ... except in the hearts of those of us who lived and played there.

So, let's get to the bottom of it - Lake Jocasse, that is. *Whippoorwill Farewell: Jocassee Remembered* is my collection of these childhood memories and photographs. Inside these covers are rare – perhaps one-of-a-kind – photographs of this beautiful Valley. Some were taken as early as 1914, long before dynamite carved out its cruel facade.

Hopelessly sentimental, I love to laugh and have absolutely no trouble crying. Maybe that's why these carefree memories of Jocassee Valley are so special to me. They spark an emotion that, for a moment, takes me back to my childhood – when everything was simple and innocent. I hope it will make *you* laugh – and perhaps cry – as you take a trip back through your own memories, recalling family times that warm your heart.

A pastor once told me that the word "remember" means "to put back together; to re-member." It is my hope that in these pages ... Jocassee will be remembered.

*Imagine being able to look through the crystal waters of
Lake Jocassee, 300 feet deep . . . here's a glimpse of
what you'd see*

Mid-April 1971.

Duke orders the tunnel diverting the Keowee River around the dam site closed.

My valley begins to drown.

The Wake

I don't recall the exact date I last saw Jocassee. I know only that the gates were going to close soon. Uncle Fred called and said they were going up one last time – he asked if I would like to come along.

I remember I was so distraught at the road's condition, gutted by all the logging trucks lumbering in and out. The dirt road was absolutely destroyed – pitted with deep potholes, rough and rugged. It was an effort to enter Jocassee by car. The Valley had been raped, and the effects were so evident.

Attakulla Lodge sat forlornly desolate. It, too, had been raped, pillaged by looters who helped themselves to whatever was of any use. Even mantlepieces had been stripped from the fireplaces. I wandered through the hallway, too heartbroken even to retrieve some token of remembrance. I watched Fred's backlit silhouette as he stood on the porch, staring at the pasture, fidgeting with some small something, turning it over and over in his fingers to absorb his grief.

We didn't say much to each other. Couldn't. It was like saying goodbye to a dying friend, but without the hope of Heaven's reunion. The Lodge was a tough ol' lady who, for half a century, had welcomed many a weary traveler. Only much later in life did I realize the impact this place would have on me.

Duke begins "clearing" the land. Vegetation close to the lake surface was removed.
At deeper depths, entire forests were left standing.
(Courtesy of Duke Power Archives)

Foreboding

A single, powdery, velvet-thick dirt road ambled through the Valley, cresting at a steep bluff overlooking the river and the domain of a long-forgotten Cherokee people. Unspoiled and practically virginal, the Valley was well-protected by mountains which rose like tremendous shoulders guarding a priceless treasure. We rarely traveled that extra mile or so past the Lodge. Other than the spectacular view, I guess there was no reason to. It would always be there.

VALLEY OF JOCASSEE, S. C.

This drawing of Jocassee Valley accompanied the
1853 Harper's New Monthly Magazine article

T. Addison Richards, in an 1853 *Harper's New Monthly Magazine* article, described Jocassee as:

> ... the fair valley of Jocassee, dissected by the babbling waters of the sparkling Keowee; the very spot to dream in on a summer-morn; or, in moonlight-hours to dance with the woodland elf and the merry fay! In connection with a visit to Jocassee, the traveler invariably "does" the proximate falls of the White Water, charming in themselves, and still more happily remembered in association with the wild beauties of the mountain ledges and dells, traversed in the few miles rambled thence, from the bosom of the pretty valley. In the same excursion, too, he will ever cherish with delight a memory of the Keowee, the silent waters of Jocassee's glens,

> > Down in thy crystal depths are seen
> > The pebble and the pearly shell,
> > Or rock with velvet robe of green,
> > Whose shade the bright trout loves so well,
> > When in the sun's unclouded beam,
> > Like silver glistens all thy stream."

> > Upon thy marge the violet blows,
> > The lily bends its snow-white head,
> > And nigh the lofty chestnut grows,
> > And flings its shadows o'er thy bed,
> > While laurels to thy ripples bend,
> > And to the air their fragrance lend."

> > Thy banks along of brightest green
> > (When summer skies above thee glow),
> > The wild deer in his pride is seen,
> > His image in the wave below;
> > And there he sips thy crystal tide,
> > Nor dreams of danger by thy side!"

But by the mid 1960s, danger had come to the Valley.

I remember the day danger came. The summer sounds were ever-present as the Whitewater River cavorted and pranced its way past Attakulla Lodge (the river carried diamonds, you know ... lots and lots of tiny, brilliant, icy diamonds that sparkled on top of the water). The swelling chorus of crickets in the later afternoon sun gladly silenced themselves at twilight in deference to the deep-throated bullfrogs ... more in an attempt to keep from being eaten than to show honor! It was a typical Jocassee day – except for the presence of the power company man.

I remember walking out onto the Lodge's huge front porch – for everything is huge from a child's perspective – and seeing a man in a white shirt talking to Uncle Buck and Mama. He was the power company man, bringing morbid news of plans to build a huge dam which eventually would envelop our valley under the shroud of a huge lake ... and leave a huge hole in our souls. While the grownups talked, I busied myself by swinging around the columns on the edge of the porch. I wish that I had understood the magic of the place, before it was too late.

But a child thinks that things will last forever.

My heart would skip a beat at this first glimpse of Attakulla Lodge as we approached. This photo was taken from "the Ford" - a somewhat shallow crossing in the river. Some dared drive across it, although there were a few deep holes to avoid, and the current was swift.

This spectacular view of the "Burgess Bottoms" awaited those who ventured to the end of the valley. Whitewater River (unseen in the foreground of this photograph) sweeps past the foot of a steep bluff and a sharp turn in the road.

A distant Lake Jocassee as seen from the brink of Upper Whitewater Falls

Heavenly Days

The Bible says that Heaven's streets are paved with gold, but the nearest place I knew to heaven on earth had a dusty road which followed every bend in the river as it wound its way into an enchanted land. A pristine valley tucked peacefully away in upper Oconee County, Jocassee's life was the Whitewater River, which told the tale of recent rains - or drought - depending on its crystal clarity or muddy torrents.

A narrow bridge with steel girders heralded the only entrance into the Valley. Crossing the bridge on our first day back to Jocassee, Mama would always note the condition of the river. "Boy, it's sure been raining! It'll take a couple of days for the river to clear up!" — or "River's low!" Pop said, "We can tell when it's really raining in the mountains. The river swells up. When it pours rain, the green waters turn into red torrents." If the river overflowed its banks by 3 or 4 feet, the road was submerged, and the valley was stranded.

The road sign announces your arrival at Jocassee,
right before the bend in the road to the steel bridge.
(Courtesy Duke Power Archives)

9

Whatever the river's condition, it was always a joy to be back! I scarcely have a childhood memory that isn't in some way linked to Jocassee Valley. We lived in Columbia, but Jocassee was our retreat — our place of refreshment — a place where we could truly relax and spend time enjoying the river, the food, the scenery.

Returning to the Valley, rounding the curve just before the steel bridge, the first thing you saw was *Camp Jocassee for Girls*. This marked the beginning of the Valley — and of my family's life there. Its anchor building was a stately two-story Victorian-like house built in the late 1890s by my Great-Grandfather, William Macajah Brown, as a home for his young wife, Sarah Louise Glazener. From Rosman, North Carolina, he and Lou traveled over the mountains by horse-drawn wagon to start a new life in Jocassee Valley ... a suitable beginning for a young couple who would raise a family of 8 children.

The "Brown House," renamed "Wallace Building," at Camp Jocassee for Girls — the original home of Granddaddy and Granny Brown around 1889. I believe this at one time was known as the "Whitewater Inn."

Camp girls sunning under the steel bridge. The bridge, which was left in place as the waters rose, has recently been located by Off the Wall Diving. Covered in approximately 5 inches of silt, it still silently guards the Valley's entrance.

Must Be Love!

Written by W. M. Brown to Sarah Louise Glazener
(A typed version follows the original letter)

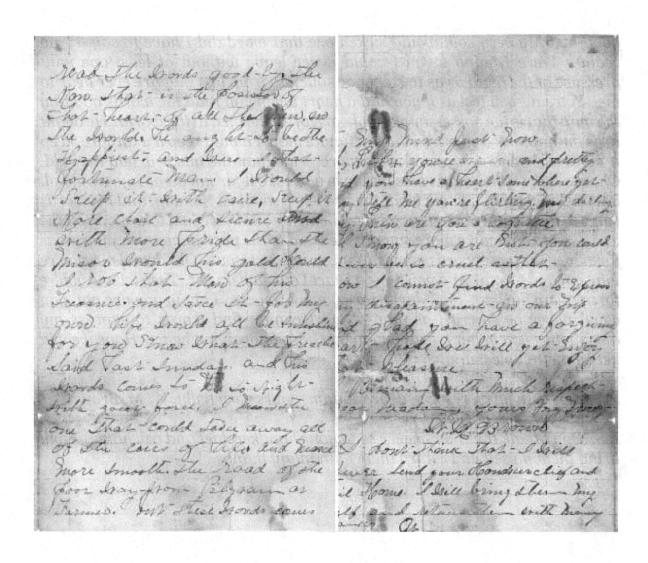

At Home
Nov 3rd 1887
Dear Miss Lou,

Your very welcome letter to hand. Was very glad to receive your kind words of sympathy. Words made doubly dear to me because of the high esteem in which I hold the author. I am glad that at least there is one that can sympathize with a poor fellow that has got the mumps, and your sympathies are appreciated highly, and received with many thanks. I feel better tonight, that is my head has stopped aching and my jaws does not hurt so bad as they did on yesterday. I hope to be well soon and once more enjoy something to eat. For let me say that I am tired of milk and mush and gruels. I'm tired of sitting in the house. The words good-bye that you now could never have been meant for one, you, I mean whose company has for me, so many charms and from whom the slightest word comes every sensation of my heart to beat with increasing rapidity. Oh, so not good-by. My very soul would sicken ore that word did I have to say it - no really. Were I going away I could never leave without at least one joint pressure of the hand or as to steal one soul kiss from lips that are ever dear to me. You said you feel as if you had a heart when you read the words good-by the man that is the possessor of that heart, of all the men in the world. He ought to be the happiest and were I that fortunate man, I would keep it with care, keep it more close and secure and with more pride than the misor would his gold. Oh, could I rob that man of his treasure and take it for my own. Life would all be sunshine, for you know what the preacher said last Sunday, and his words come to me tonight with great force. I mean the one that could take away all the cares of life and make more smooth the road of the poor way-worn pilgrim as farmer. Out these words comes to my mind just now. Oh, dear Lou, you're winsom and pretty. And you have a heart I own where yet. They tell me you're flirting, my darling. Say, darlin, are you a coquette. I know you are not, you could never be so cruel as that. Now I cannot find words to express my disappointment in our trip and glad you have a forgiving heart. Hope we will yet enjoy that pleasure.

I remain with much respect, dear Madam, yours very truly, W. M. Brown

P.S. Don't think that I will never send your handkerchief and veil home. I will bring them myself and return them with many thanks. W---

Pages from the Brown Family Bible

Parents	
W. M. Brown	May 18, 1860
Lou Glazener	May 27, 1867

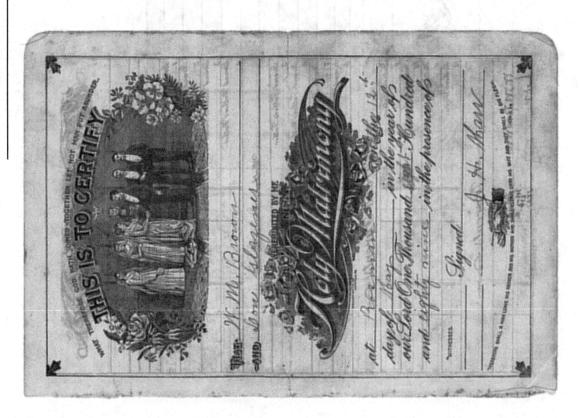

	Children		
		Born	
Names		When	Where
1. Fred Brown		April 11, 1890	N.C.
2. Arthur Brown		July 15, 1891	N.C.
3. Clyde Brown		April 25, 1894	S.C.
4. Loyd Brown		December 27, 1895	S.C.
5. Myrtle Brown		December 16, 1897	S.C.
6. Ruth Brown		February 23, 1901	S.C.
7. Grace Brown		March 11, 1906	S.C.
8. Morris Brown		July 13, 1908	S.C.

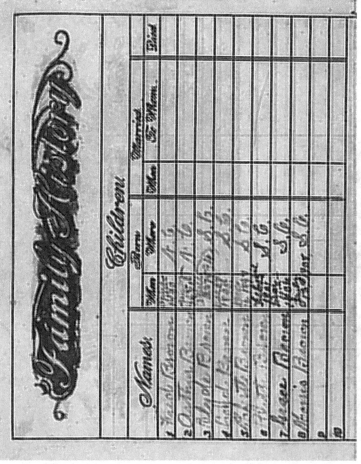

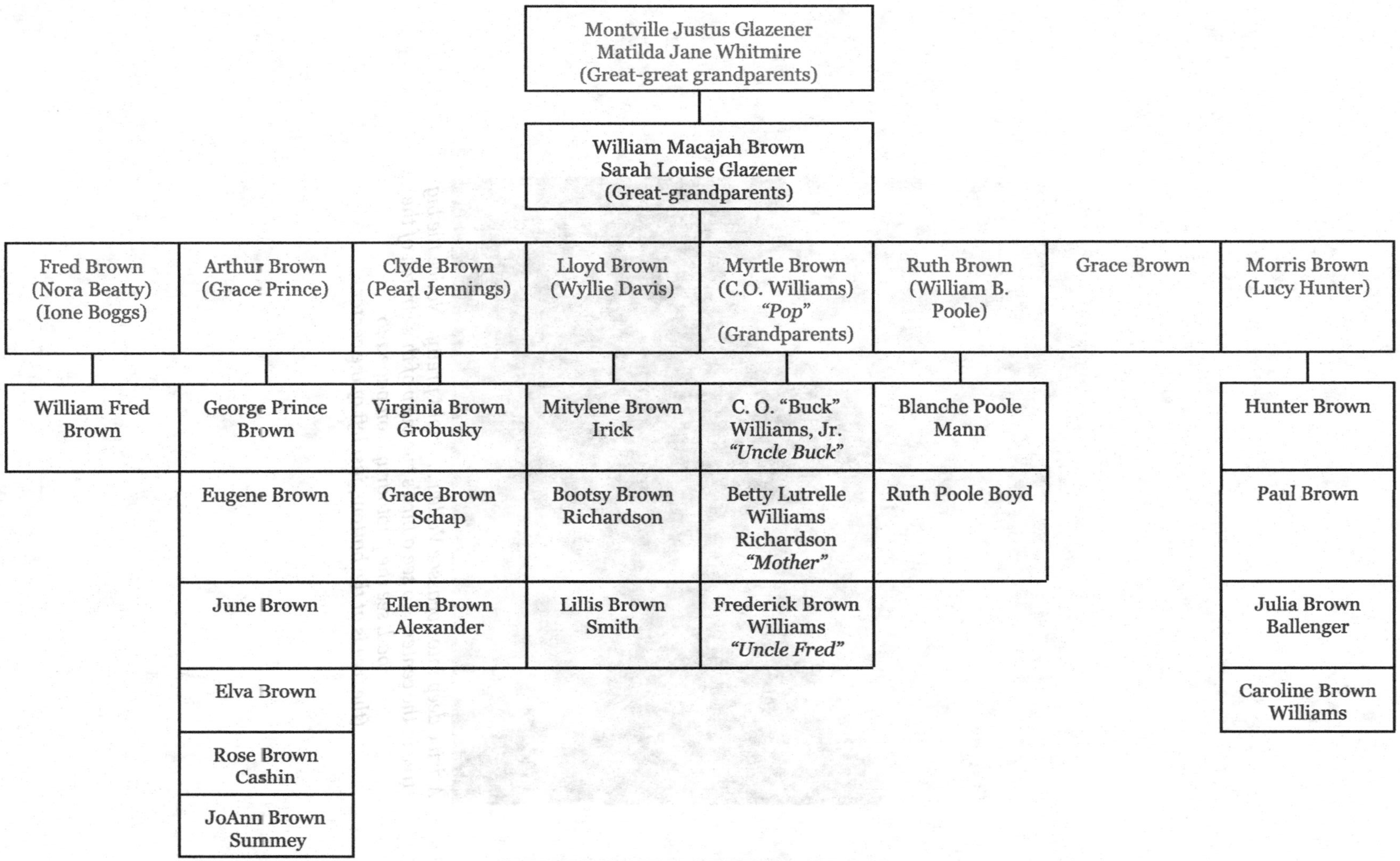

Montville Justus Glazener
Matilda Jane Whitmire
(Great-great grandparents)

William Macajah Brown
Sarah Louise Glazener
(Great-grandparents)

Fred Brown (Nora Beatty) (Ione Boggs)	Arthur Brown (Grace Prince)	Clyde Brown (Pearl Jennings)	Lloyd Brown (Wyllie Davis)	Myrtle Brown (C.O. Williams) *"Pop"* (Grandparents)	Ruth Brown (William B. Poole)	Grace Brown	Morris Brown (Lucy Hunter)
William Fred Brown	George Prince Brown	Virginia Brown Grobusky	Mitylene Brown Irick	C. O. "Buck" Williams, Jr. *"Uncle Buck"*	Blanche Poole Mann		Hunter Brown
	Eugene Brown	Grace Brown Schap	Bootsy Brown Richardson	Betty Lutrelle Williams Richardson *"Mother"*	Ruth Poole Boyd		Paul Brown
	June Brown	Ellen Brown Alexander	Lillis Brown Smith	Frederick Brown Williams *"Uncle Fred"*			Julia Brown Ballenger
	Elva Brown						Caroline Brown Williams
	Rose Brown Cashin						
	JoAnn Brown Summey						

OTHER RELATIONSHIPS TO AUTHOR:

Brother: James B. "Jimmy" Richardson, Jr. (son of Jim and Betty Richardson)

Cousins: Bucky Williams (son of Buck and Francis Williams)
Lynda, Lisa and Whitney Williams (children of Fred and Shirley Williams)

A drive deep into Jocassee Valley . . . right pretty. Notice the big tree in the center. To see a bird's eye view of this stretch of the road, see the photograph on page 146 (the tree is at the bottom, just left of the center).

Attakulla Lodge:
Jocassee's Original Bed and Breakfast

Stately though the Brown House was, it was *not* the heart of Jocassee. That honor was reserved for an enormous, rambling house known as Attakulla Lodge. The Lodge was named after Chief Attakullakulla ("Little Carpenter"), father of the legendary Princess Jocassee ("Place of the Lost One").

Mother poses behind Attakulla Lodge (the dining hall is on the bottom floor; guests rooms are up above.

In the 1920s, Granddaddy Brown purchased the Lodge from the Whitmires, who were a long-established family in the Jocassee and Keowee valleys and kin to his mother-in-law. Although the exact date on which my great-great-great grandfather Henry Whitmire, Jr., built the Lodge is unknown, it was functioning as a hotel by August, 1904. Attakulla Lodge was featured in several newspapers, such as the *Independent Anderson*, which acknowledged its notable reputation "in Oconee County, and neighboring counties" as a "very popular resort hotel located in the Jocassee Valley, some 60 feet from the blue-green Whitewater River." Escaping the heat and humidity of Atlanta, Columbia and Charleston, guests would spend entire summers at the Lodge, enjoying the delicious scenery, delicious food, delicious everything! By the 1960s, however, the Lodge had closed to guests, although interest in its accommodations was still high. In the *Independent* article, Pop was quoted as saying, "This old place holds many memories. Many people still write wanting to know if we plan to re-open the Lodge. We say no ... all those years on the railroad have tired me of the tourist business."

The Lodge (which proudly displayed the misspelled sign, 'Attakula Lodge') was two stories high – three if you counted the sleeping attic – with a huge wrap-around porch which overlooked the Whitewater River. The long dining hall stretched toward the back of the house. Once a grand old house, by the time I was old enough to form memories, Attakulla Lodge was showing her age. It was in quite a state of disrepair, with leaky broken-paned windows and torn screening in the dining room. I was told I never saw it "in its glory," but to me, it was still the most beautiful place on earth.

Mama said the Lodge had an upstairs bathroom, but I remember only the one downstairs, which was probably added long after the Lodge was built. It was a big room with a concrete floor, a toilet, sink, and a showerhead. There was no shower stall – just a showerhead on the wall in plain view. The room was really much too big for what was in it, but I suppose it was already there and was just converted into a bathroom. A wooden partition, six feet high and two feet off the floor, shielded the bathroom

Look at all the windows framing the first floor. Perfect spot to sneak a peak!

from the many windows on the outside wall. Looking back on it, privacy was just something you had to respect, for it would have been really easy to sneak a peak! When I was very young, however, I didn't use the shower. Instead, Mama would heat water on the stove and fill a galvanized washtub with warm, soapy water. I especially remember bathing this way when we stayed across the river in our log cabin. I don't really know why we didn't use the shower – I guess the novelty of bathing in a big pot made it lots of fun.

Mama and I usually slept in the back room on the left at the head of the stairs. Uncle Buck and Aunt Francis always got the front room on the left (my favorite room), and Uncle Fred and Aunt Shirley always got the front room on the right. Our room was dark and, since it wasn't on the front of the house, you couldn't hear the river as well. For convenience, Mama furnished our room with what she referred to as a "slop jar." Honestly, it didn't rival the size of a soup pot! It was made of white enamel, sat right on the floor and had no seat for comfort. Aim was important! As uncomfortable as it was, however, it sure beat fumbling around at night for the flashlight and walking downstairs to the bathroom on a frigid evening. Even in summertime, the evenings were cold, and the Lodge had no heat except for a wood stove in the kitchen. What a wonderful feeling to jump back into bed and cover up with piles and piles of handmade quilts and blankets! You never had a better night's sleep, though ... especially when it rained. The rain pattering on the tin roof and the sound of the river at your front door was better than any panacea. My, my ... what I wouldn't give for my children to experience Jocassee!

Mother holds Jimmy in front of the Lodge. The bowling alley is in spittin' distance!

For his guests' entertainment, Granddaddy Brown built a bowling alley next to the Lodge. Mama said that the pins were reset by hand and that it was great fun! Light refreshments could be purchased there, such as peanuts and a Coca-Cola (or as Mama called it – Co-Cola). Pop just called it a "dope" because he said it used to contain cocaine. The bowling alley was decorated with metal signs advertising just about anything you could want to buy – you just might not be able to get it at Jocassee. A one-room store in the Valley was *said* to be mainly a front for selling moonshine. If you wanted to purchase something substantial, you had to travel to Walhalla, Pickens, or Seneca. We rarely went into town except to go to *Gladys's Store*, located on the Jocassee side of Salem. Gladys always wore blue jeans or work pants and, typically, a man's shirt. I think she even wore some kind of work boot (long before it was fashionable for a woman to do so!). Her store wasn't much bigger than a good-sized living room, but she carried an adequate variety of staples. I remember the screen door banging shut behind me as I ran to the ice cream freezer, which contained those huge brown buckets of ice cream. Pop purchased those huge containers of ice cream from Gladys on a regular basis. Why? Because he *always* ate a MIXING bowl full of ice cream every night. Of course, he also kept a plentiful supply of soft peppermint sticks, the kind that get softer the longer

A closeup view of the bowling alley.

you leave them out.

In June 1998, Dave and I were camping at Devil's Fork State Park, and we took a side trip to Gladys's. The store is now abandoned, but I peeked in the windows and saw its new 'inventory' – abandoned vacuum cleaners of every shape and description. I couldn't resist opening the screen door one more time and hearing it *bang!* as I walked down the steps.

Thankfully, some things just don't change.

Gladys's Store, as it looked in 1998.

I Remember . . .

I remember ... playing *"Heart and Soul"* on the rusty-sounding piano in the downstairs hallway. It sounded not so much like a piano as a cross between a harpsichord and an out-of-tune country guitar! That piano survived the Toxaway Dam break in 1916, in which the first floor of the Lodge was flooded and covered with 18 inches of gooey mud.

I remember ...walking down the road by myself one afternoon and passing someone, garbed in work clothes and a hat, swinging a machete to rid the bank of kudzu in front of the house. *He* nodded and said, "Afternoon." I later asked Mama who that man was, and she laughed and said, "That was no man — that was Miss Ludie!"

I remember ... hairy, moss-covered rocks in the river, the kind that almost reached out and grabbed your toes as you made your way to the middle of the river.

I remember ... sitting on a rock in the middle of the rapids at the swimming hole and watching a fish nibble on my toe.

I remember ... splashing Aunt Francis as she waded into the river, holding up her arms in gentle protest as she said, *"Oooh, Debbie, don't wet my hair!"*

I remember ... lying across the bed in the Lodge, staring at the tiny horizontal slats that made up the walls - and wondering why they didn't look like our walls in Columbia.

I remember ... asking Bucky what his most vivid memory of Jocassee was. Without hesitation, he replied, "Sweaty men yelling at each other!" Pop, Uncle Buck, and Uncle Fred were always building something — a bridge, a road, or moving a mountain from here to there. In order to be heard over the deafening machinery, they had to shout. I remember hearing **"Whoa!"** more than a few times!

I remember ... Uncle Fred telling me that, as a boy, he hiked into the Horsepasture area with a 50-pound block of salt on his shoulders, herding cattle into the natural-rimmed canyon for free-range grazing. Although necessary for the cattle's survival, the salt licks also assured that the cows would eventually return to the same spot, making it easy to round them up.

I remember ... one rainy day playing "hot potato" with a beachball in the large foyer of the Lodge. It was tiny cousin Lynda's turn to catch the ball when Bucky leapt in front of her and snatched the ball in mid-air. She vehemently turned and yelled at him, "You big dumb bunny! You give me back my beach ball!" He did.

I'll never forget.

You Better Listen to Your Mother!

My mother died unexpectedly on July 25, 1997. The next day I went to her apartment just to sit among her things. In her tape player, I found an unlabeled cassette. It contained Mama's own words as she shared with me – one last time – some of her Jocassee memories. Since she recorded this in "conversation" style, I have edited only slightly and rearranged some things for clarity. My personal comments on her recollections are in brackets:

"This is going to be done rather haphazardly, Debbie. You'll have to sort it all out and decide what you want to use and what-not. Let me stop and make sure it's working before I go any further . . . yeah, so far it seems to be working alright. While I'm thinking about it, we'll talk about the spring house. I'm sure that it was built at the time the Whitmires had the home [*Attakulla Lodge*]. Now, I don't know when the house was built. You might be able to find out from records at the Courthouse, like you were talking about. But the spring house was a rock house that had divisions in it where they set the churns of milk, crops, and things like that down in it. It had

Billy Brown poses in front of the spring house

25

shelves around the sides to place perishables that they wanted to keep cool. They used to keep all their eggs, butter, vegetables, and that sort of thing in the summertime in it. Of course, in the wintertime, it would have frozen, so I guess you could use it as a freezer. As you remember, we used to keep watermelon and cantaloupe submerged in the waters in the spring house to get them nice and cold. It was really a unique building. I don't think it had any mortar in it. The stones were just stacked so that they would not come apart. That was a definite craft that some people had. Some of them up here in Blairsville [*can do it*]. You see fireplaces and that sort of thing [*like this*]. As a matter of fact, the fireplace here in the Lodge [*Branan Lodge in Blairsville, Georgia*] is like that — you don't see any mortar. It's definitely a talent for one who does it that well. [*Uncle Fred tells me that it did have mortar, except that it was applied on the inside of the building so it could not be seen from the outside.*] And it had screen wire right up at the very top of it, so the air could circulate. The door could be locked by a thing that turned to keep the door closed to keep the animals out of it. We used to have a picture somewhere of the springhouse, but whether that's in my box of pictures I have or not, I don't know."

"Back in the days when Mother ran the Lodge — before and during World War II — the laundry was really a problem. We used an iron washpot out beyond the back — you know, built a fire under it, boiled the clothes, then rinsed them in many waters in big, tin, galvanized tubs. I know you've seen those tubs [*yep, we used to bathe in one!*]. Of course, you didn't use your hands to take the clothes out of the washpot because it was boiling! We'd have a big, stout stick — like a broomstick — that you'd use to reach in there and get the boiling clothes out; then, trying not to get it on the ground, you would transfer 'em to the different rinse waters until you got it where it was nice and rinsed real well. It would take two people to ring out things like sheets and bedspreads in order to hang them on the lines. You would hang them as straight as you possibly could, because ironing was really hard to do back then. We had some flat irons that were kept warm on the back of the wood stove, and also some irons that had charcoal smoldering inside. But as hard as you would try to keep these irons clean, using a wood stove, you would invariably get some kind of little piece of soot or dirt or something on it and — then, there you go — ruining your nice clean things because you'd smear soot all over it while ironing. Not doing any more ironing than we did up there, we just hung the clothes out nice and straight on the line, then folded them up nice and smooth, putting them in the linen closets on top of each other as straight as you could.

When it rained, we still had to wash, unless it was a downpour — and you know we *did* have downpours up there. There was a kind of shed with a top on it that held the tubs of rinse water. We didn't hang the clothes outside, but we would take 'em up to the third floor. Now, the third floor at one time had been bedrooms, but, of course, they hadn't been used in years and years and not used as bedrooms when Mother was running the Lodge. That was a good place to hang the clothes. On the addition up over the dining room and the kitchen was screen wire up in the top of the wall [*by the ceiling*] for air circulation. Sometimes it would take 2 or 3 days for the clothes to dry thoroughly when it rained. It seemed like June and July had an awful lot of rain up there."

Attakulla Lodge in her prime, awaiting her guests

"Mother was known for her hot rolls — and I declare, they were so light that when you put 'em in your hand and closed your eyes, you couldn't even feel the roll in your hand. Sometimes she'd make as many as 200 at one sitting. She made them at nighttime. We had biscuits or cornbread for daytime meals, and hot rolls with homemade applesauce or apple butter at night. We got our apples from Uncle Arthur's place up across from the Girls Camp on the other side of the river. Well, you might say we stole them, but they would have rotted anyway, because we only picked up the ones that fell to the ground. They had trees up there which hadn't been sprayed or taken care of, so you had to cut around a lot of bruised places and worm holes to get the good out of the apple, but it really made good applesauce and apple butter. It was that kind of apple."

Hot Rolls -
½ cup lukewarm water - dissolve one yeast cake in this water - one cup scalded milk - add 4 tbs - oil 1 tbs - sugar + small amt - salt - cool to lukewarm yeast add about 4 or 5 cups sifted flour - one egg - beat till smooth - add flour till a stiff dough - pour on doughboard & knead till shiny - put in greased pan - let rise in warm place till double in size - place back on doughboard - knead again - cut small pieces & make rolls - grease pan - also grease top of rolls - set in warm place to rise double - bake at 400°.

myrtle williams' receipt for rolls she made at Greasee, S.C. "attakulla Lodge" in her hand writing - Betty Richardson, daughter

"Miss Ludie and Miss Sarah Godbold [*sisters*] ran the Camp [*Camp Jocassee for Girls*]. Miss Ludie was the gym teacher at Columbia College for women, the Methodist school there in Columbia, and Miss Sarah was the physical ed teacher at Columbia High School there in Columbia. Miss Ludie was known world-wide, I guess, because she won the discus throw in the Olympics. I don't know exactly what year it was — probably around 1927 [*it was 1922 in Paris - she won 6 medals - including a gold in the shot put and a gold in the hop-step-jump*]. They were very staunch disciplinarians, and they ran that Camp like

Miss Ludie Godbold

a top Sergeant! Maybe some of the top Sergeants could have learned from Miss Ludie and Miss Sarah. [*Miss Ludie openly admitted that when she (Ludie) died, "Sarah will be the ugliest woman on earth!"*] They loved to come to the Lodge when Mother would invite them for meals. She would have them twice during the summer season. When they first came up to clean up the Camp to get it ready for the summer, she would have them for supper one night, then again when they closed the Camp. They really looked forward to it! When she knew that Miss Ludie and Miss Sarah were coming, she'd make over 200 rolls, and I tell you, I don't think there was any left. She'd have fried chicken and all the good things that go with that. As a usual thing, the guests would seat one of these big, long tables in the dining room, and the family ate with them. I don't know exactly how many places that was, but we could figure it up by the number of bedrooms and sleeping spaces for the guests. Fred, of course, was in charge of helping to get the chickens ready, and I was, too. Mother would ring the necks of the chickens and hang them up on the clothesline in the backyard to let all the blood run out. Then it was up to us to scald and the feathers. She did the rest of it. I never did learn how to take out the intestines and do all that stuff. I don't know if I could have ever done that or not. Fred and I had to be sure they were picked clean, and that meant all the little pin feathers and everything. Unless you've really picked a chicken before, and I think you probably haven't [*how true*], it's quite a chore to get all the feathers out. Fried chicken back then at the Lodge tasted entirely different from what we get in the stores now. Fresh chicken "on their feet," or whatever you call it, just tastes differently. It's very, very good. Of course, it was very, very fresh."

"We had a gas refrigerator, but it didn't hold a whole lot — only the perishables like butter, eggs, and milk. The vegetables, like I said, were kept in baskets in the spring house. We had a big garden up there. Every spring - about April, I believe it was - Homer Whitmire sent his boys up there with their mule. I'm sure that Homer didn't do it, but the boys plowed up the garden, and they planted whatever it was that Mother wanted. I'm sure she sent money for seeds, so that the garden would have a good start by the time we got up there in June or the last of May, whenever school got out. We picked vegetables every morning while the dew was still on them to have for that day: green beans, squash, and so forth. We grew some cantaloupe, and, of course, we always had tomatoes, okra, and butterbeans. There would be fresh ones to pick every day. Anyway, the garden produced pretty good for the whole summer. If you remember, the garden area went from the kitchen back over to that first cottage [*behind the Lodge*]. It might have been an acre or more of land. I don't really have any idea how much it was. Anyway, it sure produced. That soil was very rich — nice black soil — and it had a fence around it to keep out the deer. Of course, rabbits would

Horses frolic by the old barn

get through and eat some of the stuff. We also had fresh strawberries, and we picked fresh blackberries from down there by the barn [*at the end of the pasture*]. We grew practically everything. About the only thing we bought was coffee, sugar, tea, and lard — staples, you know, such as dried beans and things like that, but all the vegetables were fresh from right there. Daddy [*Pop*] would come up on the weekends. He would go to the Farmers Market in Columbia and bring peaches when they first came into season. He came practically every weekend by "dead-heading" on the railroad. He could ride free, you know, and would bring these things in the baggage car. He would bring whatever he thought Mother could use. Sometimes when weeks were slack (a lot of people came on weekends but not many during the week), the fresh produce that was left over would be canned for us to use back in Columbia during the wintertime. When she was physically able, Granny Brown did a lot of canning. She had a tremendous garden, also, in Walhalla."

"Uncle Morris was famous for making sausage. Granddaddy had hogs on his farms. He owned quite a few farms around Oconee and Pickens Counties. Morris would kill the hogs, then "render the lard" (I believe that's what they called it). They'd boil the fat and make the lard. But his sausage! He not only used the spare parts that couldn't be cooked and made into roasts and hams, like most people did, but Uncle Morris would use all the hog. He would use the hams, the shoulders, everything, so his sausage was really nice and lean. He seasoned it — oh, it was so good!

Uncle Morris as a young man

When we fried up the sausage, Mother had these great big iron frying pans. I don't know whatever happened to them, but they must have been 2-3 feet in diameter. It would take both hands to pick up one. I'm tellin' you, they were heavy, heavy, heavy. They would fire up the wood stove and fry up I-don't-know-how-many patties of sausage at one time. Granny had all these big glass jars that must have held 2 or 3 gallons apiece. They had wide mouths to them, so that you could put the sausage down into these jars and, after your grease cooled off, you'd pour it over the sausage until it got hard or congealed. It was like canning. You could keep sausage indefinitely that way. Then, after hog-killing time, you always had sausage. It was really handy to have there at the Lodge. To cook that many breakfasts every morning, you wouldn't have time to sit there by the stove and fry out all the sausage that was needed, along with eggs and grits and make biscuits. The sausage also came in good to take back to Columbia. We'd have sausage all winter, taking it out of those big jars. Granny did a lot of that, too, in Walhalla. I'm sure a lot of the sausage came from there. Uncle Morris would take the uncooked sausage to her, and she would do them up. He cured hams, too, and he did a real good job of that. He made country ham, not smoked ham. A lot of people had smoke houses, but they didn't have a smoke house up there. There might have been one there at one time, though. They would cure the hams by hanging them up probably in dark rooms, and season them with salt and pepper."

Mother and Fred

"People really knew how to live back in those days, but it was hard work for a woman who had to practically spend her entire day in the kitchen doing nothing else but preparing food and putting it away for the winter for the family. Mother grew herbs out in the garden, also, so she used fresh herbs in her cooking. I must say, not because she was my mother, but she was one of the best cooks I have ever encountered to meet. Her food was seasoned so good, and she made such beautiful pastries and cakes. She didn't even have a mixer until after World War II; yet she would make these beautiful cakes. When we made coconut cake, though, oh, I dreaded that!! Buck dreaded it! Fred dreaded it! We all dreaded it! First of all, you'd have to get the shell off the coconut and then, where the coconut has the 3 eyes, you would punch these with an ice pick or something, so that you could drain the milk out. Then you had to crack the coconut, cut the brown off, then grate it. I must say that a lot of the cakes and stuff that had coconut in them probably had half of our knuckles, also. All we had was an old-timey grater, you know, where you grated back and forth, so needless to say, we didn't have coconut cake very often at the Lodge. Mother would fix it some in Columbia. She made delicious pies and cobblers. Her pastry was, oh, out of this world! I think about it now — if she had lived in a later era, we could have had a frozen food factory that would have been out of this world — put Sarah Lee out of business!"

"Mother usually hired 2 high school girls from Walhalla to work at the Lodge during the summer. They were from relatively poor families. Their parents were probably glad to have them away from home, because it was one less mouth to feed. She paid something like $15.00 a week, plus room and board. They helped with the house cleaning, dish washing, and food preparation — like scrubbing carrots, peeling potatoes, all that sort of thing. They also helped with the washing. We ALL worked. Nobody up there could be a slouch. Everybody had to work. Back then, I guess $15.00 a week, room and board, was pretty good. Besides that, the girls had a good time. Back home, they were probably glorified babysitters and didn't have the good things to eat that we had at the Lodge. Usually while the girls were up there, Mother would sew for them. She had a pedal machine. When times were slack or it was raining, or if we didn't have many guests, she would make clothes for them — dresses. They really appreciated that. They all loved Mother very much. We'd get around the old piano — you remember how tin-panny it sounded. That was because of the Toxaway Dam breaking — I've forgotten what year it was [1916]. The water came up into the Lodge almost to the second floor. It covered that piano, and that's why it always sounded like that. You could spend any amount of money having it tuned, but it didn't do any good. It always had that tin-panny, honky-tonk sound. We'd get around the piano for recreation and sing hymns and "The Good Ship Lollipop." I can remember Aunt Ruth, who

Mother poses in the front yard of the Lodge. The beautiful Whitewater River flows in the background.

died when I was 10 or 11. She played the piano beautifully and had a beautiful singing voice, as Mother did. I can remember her playing and singing "On the good ship Lollipop" . . . you remember that song? You probably don't [*yes, I do!*]. I haven't heard it in years! But anyway, Shirley Temple sang it in a movie, and it was real popular. But that was our recreation — singing and dancing a jig around the piano. You mentioned about someone up there coming and playing the guitar and the banjo on Saturday nights, square dancing on the porch. [*In* Journey Home, *Jimmy Cornelison quoted Roy Elrod as saying that he and his musicians had a seven-year tenure at "Mr. Brown's Hotel in Jocassee, where we'd get the door (admission price) at 50 cents a couple."* Jackson and Hembree's Keowee *recalls: "The cool porches, the scenery, the abundant food cooked by mountain women and the parties and frolics with dancing and good string bands drew vacationers from everywhere. For some, nothing would stand in the way of a good time. They had a dance about every Saturday, at the upper hotel. One time there was a man got up to dance and he danced so big that he lost the button on his britches. He danced right on, and his britches fell down. He just took off his hat and held it in front of him and danced backward, right out the door."*]. I imagine the bootlegger up the road kept the people's "spirits" up. They kept going out to the car for a drink. Granddaddy wouldn't let anybody drink on the place if he knew it, but I guess he didn't always know it. I think he was kinda naive, like me."

"Granddaddy built the log cabin across the river back in the '30's, I think, during the Depression. It was built from timber, of course, cut from our mountains, and he did it more or less to keep his people busy. He had sharecroppers and other people who worked for him. You had to pay them whether they worked or not, so much a year, so if they didn't have chores — if the crops were already laid by, or the cotton was picked, he would bring them up there to peel the logs and get ready to build the house. He really built it for Mother but, as it turned out, money was very scarce during the Depression, as you well know. Now, Granddaddy had a lot of property, but he didn't have a whole lot of ready cash. In fact, he hardly ever had a lot of ready cash. He rented this cottage for something like $15.00 a month, which was considered good rent, I think.

3 of the rental cabins

He rented it to a woman who was probably in her 60's. I thought she was pretty old, but she was pleasantly plump, we'll say, and she dyed her hair red. I always thought she had very pretty clothes (ha-ha!). Oh, she dyed her stockings to match every outfit she wore, and she always carried an umbrella. Well, it turned out — and Granddaddy didn't know if for the longest kind of time — that she was a *madam!!* She had a brothel in that house up there and sold bootleg whiskey! We always wondered why she had so much company, especially on the weekends. The people would park their cars in the parking lot of the Lodge, and most of the people were men, you know. But some of them would come down and spend the night; then they'd come get in the river and play with all of us and acted just like everybody else. I'm sure they came up there to see the ladies. There must have been 2 or 3 there, and she had a very nice car for that time. It was a big old car with a running board and all that stuff. She was always asking Granddaddy every time they came in to bring ice on the trucks when they would come . . . [tape over]. We never got a renter after that who paid their rent on time, but that was funny because he had no idea what she was doing."

34

"I think the bootlegger [*Mama told me not to mention the name!*] probably had more money than most of the people up there in the mountains. But those people didn't think they were doing anything wrong, you know, by bootlegging. They use to, before the days of airplanes flying over to spot things — find revenuers to come up there and walk the mountains — men with big, tall boots on, of course, to keep from getting snake bit, looking for stills. I don't know how many times they found stills on Granddaddy's property. They'd come over and say, "Well, Mr. Brown, we found a still up here on your property on such-and-such a creek way back in the mountains, and we busted it up," they'd say. But it wouldn't be any time after that when they'd be back up there looking again and found another one, so all of these mountain people believed that it was perfectly alright to use anybody's land they wanted to put a still on, as long as it was hidden — that they had that right and that privilege, and you really shouldn't mind if they used your property for a still. But Granddaddy, being a Christian man, did not like that, and if he ever found out about one, he would report it, even if it was on his land. I guess some of that still goes on. They say it does up here. I guess things like that don't change too much. I guess some bootleggers have a reputation of making clean moonshine, although Uncle Morris told us one time that he came upon a still in the mountains. I don't know whose still it was, but the mash was curing, or whatever it does, and had dead snakes in it. They wouldn't take them out or anything. They'd just let them be in there! Can you imagine drinking something like that? I guess a lot of people probably died from stuff like that."

"I told you about the time that my first cousins June and George (Arthur's sons who were two years younger than me), and Buck killed a snake down the road — a poisonous snake. I don't know if it was a mocassin or rattlesnake. But, anyway, they thought this would be real funny. There were a bunch of us up there — my first cousin Blanche Poole from Greenville, who later married a lawyer and has a son who is a lawyer, too (Fletcher Mann) — she and her sister, Ruth, who was 2 years younger than Blanche, were all up there [*at Jocassee*]. I think Bootsy and Mitylene Brown (Lloyd's daughters) from Seneca were up there, too. The boys thought it would be real funny if they put the snake in the bed that Blanche and I slept in, there in the front room off the front porch, and see what happened when we got in bed that night. Well, that night we got in bed, and the boys were coming in and out of the room looking and peering, wondering what was going to happen. Nothing happened — no screaming or carrying on. They finally could not stand it, and they pulled the covers back, and there was no snake in the bed. That snake had just been stunned, I guess, and it crawled off. But I tell you what. Mother was so mad she just about had a caniption fit, and she got a switch, and she switched not only Buck, but she switched June, and she switched George. I think she sent a note into town to their mother, Aunt Grace, and told her that she had switched them good and what they had done. Aunt Grace sent her a note back, and she said that was perfectly alright — that Mother had the authority to do whatever she wanted to do. As long as the children were up there, she was responsible for them, and if she wanted to whip 'em every day, she had her permission! We looked all over that house for that snake. They never did find anything.

Blanche Poole (left)
Bootsy Brown (center)
Betty Williams (right)

An adorable, girlish trio!

Mother, oh Lord, she was beside herself. I think that was one of the few times in her life I ever saw her mad! That was a very serious thing, but the boys thought the snake was dead, and they just thought we'd reach down there with our feet and touch it and "YYYIIIIIIII!" They thought that would be a funny joke, but it wasn't very funny. Anyway, we were always doing crazy things — I mean, having a good time — riding horses and falling off of horses. I don't think the rest of the girls liked to ride as much as I did. I don't remember Bootsy and Mitylene riding very much, or Sis or Blanche either one. But I liked to ride. We always had a pony there in Columbia. I guess that's why I liked to ride so much. Maybe I had more experience than they had in that area. But Buck and Frederick were the ones who could really ride, and Frederick could outride any of us. He could ride bareback better than any Indian who ever lived. He wouldn't even bother to put the saddle on. He would just gallop off. He really was good."

"We were always trying to fish in the river. But right in front of the Lodge must have been the home of some turtles — big turtles — because every time we put a line in there, we'd pull up a turtle and, of course, they were too heavy for the line, and the line would break and all that stuff. To tell you the truth, I don't ever remember catching a fish. Maybe in this particular place the turtles were eating them all, although a lot of people came up there to fish. Whether they got any or not, I don't know, until the [Walhalla] Fish Hatchery started stocking the rivers. I don't know if they were doing that back then or not, when we were children. I certainly don't think they were doing it during the War." [*Bootsy Brown Richardson, Mother's cousin, told me an interesting story about a trout. During the summer, the cousins would sleep on cots on the screened-in porch at the Lodge. Bootsy was awakened during the night by cousin June, who lightly tapped her on the shoulder. When she looked up, she was face-to-face with a beautiful rainbow trout, freshly caught, still breathing. She said it was a most memorable moment seeing the moonlight glisten on the iridescent creature. June Brown died a hero in World War II when the Bridge at Remagen collapsed on him after he saw his men to safety.*]

"The highlight of the day was when the mailman came about 10:00 in the morning [*Star Route, Salem, SC*]. We had a big mailbox out by the front, and that's when you got your newspaper and whatever mail you were getting — catalogs, and that sort of thing."

"We drove into town at least once a week — took the truck in. Well, actually, as I remember, Daddy didn't get the truck until after World War II because you couldn't get a car from the time the war started. All the cars were confiscated by the government and used in the Army and Navy, and cars were not manufactured because they were manufacturing airplanes, tanks, and jeeps. If you didn't have a car, that was just too bad. You couldn't get tires, either, because rubber came from South America. They didn't have synthetics then, and so many of the ships were sunk that were bringing in supplies. Tires were scarce — very scarce — and all of them went to war for jeeps and trucks and all the things that required tires. I think we had one old second-hand car after another to use up there in the summertime. Maybe Morris had a little truck, because we used to get 200 pounds of ice every week. They would cover it with canvas, but a lot of it melted before you got back. There was a great big, homemade icebox out there in the hall, and that's where the cold drinks were kept, and the ice for iced tea was also gotten off of that piece of ice. We had to *chip* ice. If you remember Jimmy's coffee table I had cut down, which I brought from the dining room up there at the Lodge, I took it to this man to have it fixed for Jimmy. I told him, "This table is over 100 years old, I'm sure." It was an old kitchen table made out of poplar or something like that. It was no fine wood or anything, but I wanted it stained Walnut, and I told him, "I'm sure you can give it a distressed look, or rather I don't think you'll have to do that because I'm sure it's already distressed enough." He laughed about it when he brought it back to me and said, "Mrs. Richardson, it had 5 different pieces of oil cloth on it that had been thumb-tacked underneath it, and you're right … it didn't have to be distressed. I think your people were sticking ice picks in it!" Oh, and

Mother sits on top of Buck's old car. At one time, he painted "All girls who smoke, put your butts in here." His mother made him take it off. (Sorry, I couldn't resist!)

I remember we had a pan — an enamel pan, I think it was — on that table, and you'd take the ice pick and chip the ice for iced tea. That table was something else, but I think it made Jimmy a right pretty coffee table. Besides being an antique, it's very distressed looking. Anyway, that came from Jocassee — and the washstands."

"During the War, when Buck was a Cadet at the Citadel and after he got his commission, the boys would have to do so much flying time, and they would fly over the mountains at Jocassee and buzz us. You could really hear 'em coming, and you knew it was them because nobody else ever flew an airplane over there during that time. They would land in Greenville, and we would have to get in the car and somebody would have to go over to Greenville and pick 'em up and bring 'em back. They would spend the weekend up there. They did that in Columbia, too, even when Buck wasn't there. A lot of them used to come. I think the drawing card was Mother's cooking. Mother charged only $5.00 a day, room and board, up there at the Lodge. Of course, it was wartime, and I told you what a problem it was to wash clothes. The sheets were changed on the bed only once a week. They were given so many towels a week, and if they got them dirty, it was

Mother, Buck, and Myrtle at Parents Day at the Citadel. Mother was proudly wearing a suit and hat her mother made for her!

up to the guests to wash their own towels out and hang them up to dry. They couldn't get any more. $5.00, even back then, was cheap for room and board. I mean, a lot of places you could get a meal for 35 or 50 cents, but not liked Mother fixed food. She put it on the table, and they ate as much as they wanted. And I tell you what's the truth, some of those people could eat like it was going out of style. I remember this one man who, when the chicken was passed, he'd put 4 or 5 pieces on his plate at one time, just like he wasn't ever going to have anything else to eat again! It became known for Mother's good cooking, and I think a lot of the traveling salesmen came on weekends, you know. They were too far from home, and, of course, there was a gas shortage and rationing, so they didn't have the gas to go back home. If they were in the territory, they would come there and stay for the weekend. And they ate like it was going out of style. They probably made money on an expense account by doing so. It was $5.00 a day for 3 FULL cooked meals, and I mean FULL . . . I'm telling you the truth. But everyone seemed to have a good time, and we had a big old bell that was used at Granny Brown's in the day when she had her family and all up there. That was the signal to come to the table. Mother would usually ring it 5 minutes before she meant that the food would be ready on the table so it would be nice and hot. They could get to the table, and then she'd put the food out. I don't know whatever happened to that bell. Somebody stole it one year when we went home. We should have put it up, because Granddaddy and Granny probably had it when they kept boarders. Granny had boarders up at the Brown House when Mother was born, where the Camp later was. She kept boarders in the summertime, too. Granddaddy would go in with the wagon, and Granny would pack food in trunks, if you can imagine that, because it would take a full day to take the wagon into Seneca, and then he would spend the night and bring the trainload of people — however many people he had to bring back to the Brown House. It would take another 12 hours to bring them all back; so he had to have food for them because they would stop on the way and have a picnic. There were people who came from Atlanta and what not who stayed all summer. They moved from the Brown House when Mother was 5 years old [*around 1903*]. They moved into town [*Walhalla*]."

The Browns in their Walhalla home, Christmas of 1922

Enjoy!

The dining hall (for it was much bigger than a dining *room*) was the largest room in Attakulla Lodge, well-suited for serving the many guests who spent their summers there. The tables were hand-made and spanned half the length of the room. They were so unique, in fact, that in *Keowee* Jackson and Hembree referred to the Lodge as "... the old Whitmire place, where there was a long dining table with lots of chairs." In my child's mind, I was sure we could have seated hundreds of people at that table!

We always ate supper at the same time each night, and it was a feast from anyone's point of view — food the likes of which I have never had since. We knew nothing of fat grams nor the perils of fried foods. Who cared about the calories contained in the rich, fattening desserts! The cornbread was to die for — extra crunchy because it was baked in an iron skillet and loaded with fresh butter. The chicken was fresh and fried (fresh, meaning FRESH! — if you know what I mean). Cobbler was made from the giant, sweet and succulently-juicy blackberries we picked from the bushes which grew wild at the end of the pasture. We usually brought back a few chiggers with us, so Mama would always make me take a bath in Octagon soap after picking blackberries. (I mistakenly thought that she made me bathe in *lye* soap. Through her chuckles, she informed me if that were the case, I'd have no skin left!) If that didn't kill the chiggers, a dab of fingernail polish would do the trick. Judging from the smell, though, I don't see how anything could live after being cured in Octagon soap.

After supper, everyone headed out to the front porch to grab a rocking chair. There was plenty of porch and lots of rockers. We'd just sit in the dark and listen to the river rush to greet the bullfrogs. I can close my eyes and still hear the shuffle of our shoes on the wooden porch and the *bang!* of the screened door as the last of the dishwashers (all dishes were washed by hand, of course) made their way to the porch.

One night, it was Bucky and Jimmy's turn to wash dishes. The next night, while setting the table, Mama and Aunt Shirley noticed that the "clean" plates were still dirty. As it turns out, the boys had washed the plates only on one side . . . the side you eat off of!

Mouthwatering Memories

Pop had an old, black pickup truck with benches built along the inside of the truck bed. Every day, we kids pestered the daylights out of any grownup around, begging for a ride down to the swimming hole. A wide, deep bend in the river, complete with a sandy beach and a few rapids, the swimming hole was about a mile or so down the road from the Lodge.

Cousin Lynda scoots past Pop's old pickup truck

When we were old enough, we were allowed to float down to the swimming hole from the Lodge on honest-to-goodness black, patched inner tubes. I can still hear the *slap!* of the inner tubes as they were tossed into the river! After an afternoon in the exhilarating mountain water, someone would meet us at the swimming hole with the pickup. We'd tromp up the hill, pile in the back of the truck, and go back to the Lodge.

Our appetites were enormous after river-romping in that frigid water, and we'd head to the spring house behind the Lodge and haul up an icy-cold watermelon. Uncle Buck or Uncle Fred would split it open, and we'd dive in — face and all! No forks for us. I'm surprised we didn't have a watermelon patch in front of the Lodge, given all the seeds we spit out by the steps. I can see the headlines now: *Mysterious Vine Choking Waters of Lake Jocassee* – not hydrilla, but green, bulbous fruit breaking the surface, snagging skiers.

One afternoon Uncle Fred had more than watermelon on HIS mind. It was no secret that one of his favorite desserts was lemon meringue pie, and Mama had made one the night before. He hid his piece on the shelf way back in the pantry. Apparently he didn't do a very good job, though, because when he came in from swimming — his mouth waterin' like the river — he discovered that Aunt Shirley had downed his piece of pie!

Mama said he almost cried. She had to bake another pie just for her little brother.

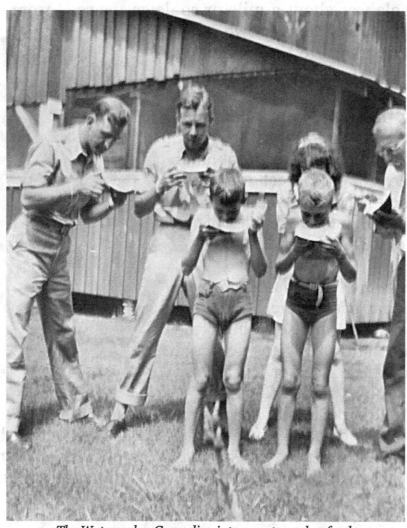

The Watermelon Gang digs into a watermelon fresh
from the spring house . . . behind the Lodge. Uncle Fred's the skinny
little fellow on the right!

If It'd Been a Snake ...

Snakes were very common at Jocassee. We had the usual — black snakes, rattlesnakes, copperheads, and water moccasins ... B-I-G ones ... snakes as big as a fireman's hose!! I was always reminded to stay away from the banks of the river, but nobody ever told me to watch out for them on the bridge, too!

Pop, Buck, and Fred built a wooden car bridge across the Whitewater River. The bridge was secured on each end by steel cables anchored to large trees and just skimmed the surface of the water. One day, I was

skipping across the bridge ahead of my cousin, Becky, when suddenly she started *screaming*! Terrified, I turned to see what was the matter, and she pointed to a huge water mocassin just slithering into the water. He had been coiled up, sunning himself on the bridge ... *and I jumped right over him.* The way we took off running back to the cabin would make you think he was chasing *us*! He was probably halfway to the swimming hole and just as eager to get away from two crazy girls.

The car bridge, as seen from the swinging bridge. Notice the chicken wire showing on the photograph. Our mothers insisted chicken wire be put on the sides of the swinging bridge to keep us kids from falling into the river!

Years later, Barbara Smith, a life-long friend, said that the one thing that stuck with her about Jocassee is my telling her not to go down to those bridges alone! Obviously, the memory of that snake stuck with me!

Mother has a good laugh while dangling her feet in the river. There were not many unhappy times at Jocassee! You can tell there had been a lot of rain from the debris washed up underneath the bridge, obviously buckling it.

Aren't You Glad That Cows Can't Fly!

The pasture served a dual purpose — obviously, as a grazing place for the cows and horses — but also as a place for Uncle Buck to land his plane! A fast-food restaurant in a small North Georgia town displays a raised relief map of the area as it appeared in the early 1960's. Yes, there is a tiny black airplane on the map, right at the intersection of Devils Fork Creek and Whitewater River — exactly on the runway of *Jocassee International Airport*!

Naturally, caution had to be exercised when landing. A careful approach was critical in order to avoid the power lines at the end of the pasture, and it always helped to "buzz" the field to scatter the cows and horses before landing. And anyone who's ever landed a plane in a cow pasture knows that you must watch where you step when getting off the plane!

Two incidents are *etched in my mind* regarding our flights to Jocassee. Excitement was the theme for the day when Uncle Buck flew into Columbia to take us to Jocassee. I remember one morning my mother tried desperately to get me to eat breakfast before we left. I couldn't choke down a bite. Unfortunately, the ride was unusually turbulent, as anyone who has ever flown in a small airplane knows it can be, and ... well, let's just say that I doubt Aunt Francis ever wore that scarf again after I was through with it!

On his last trip to Jocassee before leaving for Vietnam, Uncle Buck borrowed a single-engine plane from a friend. Because of the power lines and the short length of the pasture, it was necessary almost to stall the plane in order to land. Unfortunately, we hit a sudden gust of wind which set the plane too far down the runway. The morning dew was still on the grass, which effectively caused the plane to slide as if on ice. Braking was useless. Bucky, acting co-pilot, dutifully reported, "We're going too fast," to which Uncle Buck simply replied, "*Shut up.*" Not having enough power in a single-engine plane to make another approach, Uncle Buck was forced to stop the runaway plane before the propane tank at the rapidly-approaching end of the pasture did it for him. A last-second ground loop – an emergency U-turn – spun the plane around and stopped it, barely avoiding catastrophe. I was in the back seat between Mama and Aunt Francis — listening to them pleading with God for help — looking from one face to the other and not knowing what in the world was going on. The only damage from our near-miss was a bent landing gear — unless you want to count the near-heart attack my step-grandmother Exie almost had when she saw an airplane barreling towards the Lodge at breakneck speed! Mama threw her hands up and said, "Oh, thank you, Lord!" Aunt Francis replied, "How about give Buck a little credit!" I remember watching Uncle Buck take off the next day to Anderson for repairs.

Cleared for landing at Jocassee International!

Timber!!

Landing an airplane in a cow pasture is tricky. Landing while dodging power lines and a persimmon tree is trickier.

Homer Whitmire owned the land adjacent to the end of the pasture ... and Homer Whitmire owned the persimmon tree right in Buck's flight path. Buck approached Homer to make a deal.

"I'll give you $100 for that persimmon tree."

Well, $100 was nothing to sneeze at, but Homer refused to sell, perhaps hoping for a better offer. In the meantime, the rains poured, and the stream running between the two properties overflowed its banks ... toppling the persimmon tree.

Homer told Buck he reckoned he'd take $100 for that tree. Buck – true business man he was – said a fallen persimmon tree didn't do him any good.

Apparently, during the last 35 years, that story has made the rounds and become a local legend. Jimmy was recently at a gas station in Salem and happened to meet Mr. Tally, who perked up and asked if he had ever heard the story of the persimmon tree. Jimmy listened as Mr. Tally began to spin the yarn.

Funny. I had never heard that story before.

W. M. Brown surveys his Jocassee property

A Cup of Joe's WHAT?

There was an old-timer named Joe who lived in the valley. He delighted in greeting Uncle Buck as he landed the airplane. Buck kept asking Joe if he wanted to take a ride in the plane, and Joe'd reply, "As long as I can keep one foot on the ground!" I guess Buck's determination paid off, because Joe finally agreed to a flight around the valley.

During the trip, Buck spotted a wisp of smoke curling lazily up out of the trees. He circled around to take another look and thought he spotted something that looked a lot like a still!

"Joe, I think there's a still down there!"

"No, ain't no still down there."

"Yeah, I'm pretty sure that's a still."

"No, it's just a bunch o' campers."

Buck replied, "Maybe I should radio Greenville about this!"

"Don't bother with that ... just a bunch o' campers!"

Buck grinned and replied, "Well, if that's a still, I bet they make some *&%!# fine white lightnin'!"

The next morning, a half gallon jug of white lightning anonymously appeared on the doorstep of Attakulla Lodge.

At first glance, one might think this to be just a pretty valley scene. However, since I obtained this photo from Duke's archives, I wondered about its significance. It was evident to me, after searching through 10,000 or so photos of the Jocassee project, that Duke did not take a picture of something that had no significance to the project. I believe this is a shot of the two mountains between which the Jocassee dam would be built. If you compare the tree line of the mountain on the right to the same view on page 137, you will see they appear to be the same - only the angle from which the picture was taken is different.

Flyin' Fire

Boys! I don't think I'll ever completely understand them.

Being a typical little sister, I did quite a good job of trying to follow Jimmy and Bucky around. As a general rule, they were equally as good at eluding me ... especially when they were up to something.

One of their passions was building model airplanes – painstakingly monitoring each detail.   When finished, they would then march up to the 2nd or 3rd floor of the Lodge and launch the planes out the window, only to watch each one land in a thousand splinters. We're talking about BIG models. I never could see the point in throwing something out the window — *sometimes set on fire*, no less — and watching it crash to the ground. Fortunately, I have a picture to prove it!

Look out below!

You Can't Kon a Liki!

Eventually, Jimmy and Bucky allowed me to take part in one of their "projects" — the *Kon-Liki*!

They fashioned a raft of wood scraps, hinged on the ends for transporting and girded underneath with inner-tubes. One sunny day, Jimmy agreed to take me for a ride on the *Kon-Liki* down river to the swimming hole. We sat on the raft and enjoyed the sights, dangling our feet over the side into the cold river water. It was rare to meet anyone else in the river, but that day we ran into a couple. They greeted us by saying they had just seen a snake in the water. Jimmy and I looked at each other and *casually* pulled our feet out of the water and sat Indian-style on the raft.

Nah ... we weren't afraid!

My brother, Jimmy, writes:

The old lodge, longing nostalgically for its dignified good-old-days. As you can see, my grandfather is a sort of a junk-collector. Leaning on the porch is the raft 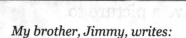 Kon-Liki, constructed by Bucky and me, and supported in the water by inner-tubes on the underside!

Might As Well Be Boot Camp

I desperately wanted to attend *Camp Jocassee for Girls*, but for years I just wasn't old enough.

I wanted to be just like the big girls who rode their horses past the Lodge every afternoon. When I heard the muffled *clip-clop* of horses, I'd scurry to the front bank which overlooked the road, so I could wave at them as they rode by. Finally, in the summer of 1966, Mama enrolled me at the Camp for a month of fun — or so I thought.

Looking back, I realize that Camp Jocassee was a *dream* for lots of girls — but I was miserable! I was terribly homesick for the Lodge, and seeing Mama drive up and down the dirt road and honk her horn in front of the Camp didn't help. I was "short-sheeted" on my first night (why *ME?*) and assigned KP the first week, to boot. Shy and chubby, I took all this much too personally.

My Dream

The final straw came when I found out that I was too young to ride the horses down the road. I was devastated. I begged Mama to let me come home. The camp director said that I would be "ruined for life" if Mama gave in and let me leave early, but Mama said she'd risk it. I only stayed a week, instead of an intended month.

Looking back on it, I probably shoulda' stayed, but I had realized that, for me, Jocassee meant being at the Lodge and having the river mostly to myself. I apologize to all the young ladies who wouldn't trade their Camp Jocassee memories for anything, but I viewed the herds of girls galloping down to the swimming hole

My reality ... but still cherished memories.
Uncle Fred holds the reigns.

in the afternoon as being an extreme invasion of my space! "Oh, rats, here come the camp girls!" My only consolation was that they had to PAY to be there, and somehow I thought I had an inherent right. I understand that another resident Jocassee girl felt the same way.

It was, after all, our valley.

Jimmy lends a hand.
Poor little pony looks like he's got a load!

Uncle Buck gives me a ride!

56

Dear Daddy,

Hi! Camp hasn't been much fun yet. I guess it will be more fun when we start our activities.

Today we made out our schedules. I'm not very happy with mine. Swimming is ~~classed~~ in Junior, Intermediate, and Advanced. I would be in Intermediate, but horse-back riding will interfere with it, so I'll have to take Advanced.

The only subjects I am taking are tumbling, arts & crafts, twirling, swimming, horse riding, dancing, & chorus. I have Tuesday & Thursday afternoons when I won't have anything to do.

I asked my counselor, Shirley. Brown, if I could stay in my cabin those afternoons. She said they may make me take something to fill up those afternoons.

My cabin is "Hester". It's not very nice. Some of the girls I don't like. But, I'd better start liking them. because I have to live with them for a month. Right now they are fussing about which way to wear a bathing suit. Oh. Brother!

Well, got to go now!

Love, Debbie

P.S. Write soon!

*The following pages are reproductions of a
Camp Jocassee for Girls
Brochure*

Camp Jocassee
for Girls

IN THE CAROLINA BLUE RIDGE MOUNTAINS

CAMP JOCASSEE FOR GIRLS

MR. AND MRS. WALTER L. FOY, *Directors*
209 Oak Street
QUITMAN, GEORGIA

Post Office   Railway Station
Star Route   SENECA, S. C.
SALEM, S. C.

THE FOY FAMILY

DEAR PATRON:

Camp Jocassee, having been founded in 1922, is one of the oldest camps for girls in operation today. The individual and her development are of the utmost importance to us at Camp Jocassee, and the camp is held to a moderate size in order that those needs may be met by our staff.

We feel that we have the understanding and love for children which will bring happiness and development to any child attending our camp. We will provide safe experiences under trained supervision.

Giving your child the opportunity of actually living and adjusting to members of her society will undoubtedly prepare her for a more wholesome adult life.

We cordially invite you to give these experiences to your child at Camp Jocassee.

Sincerely,
MR. AND MRS. WALTER L. FOY

SHOWING LAWN, PART OF LAKE, WALLACE BUILDING AND CORNER OF GODBOLD HALL

STEEL BRIDGE OVER WHITEWATER RIVER

Camp Jocassee is located on the beautiful Whitewater River in the Jocassee Valley in the heart of the old Indian country. Although in South Carolina, it is five miles from the North Carolina line, about thirty-five miles from Brevard, N. C. The most available railway point is Seneca, S. C. It is on the main line of the Southern Railway from Washington to New Orleans.

Although Camp Jocassee has the valley almost to itself, there are many places of scenic and historic interest nearby. Among these are: Tamassee, the last home of General Andrew Pickens, Lover's Leap, Whitewater Falls, Sapphire and Fairfield Lakes, Cashiers' Valley, and High Hampton.

Wallace Building is the central building of camp. It is equipped with water, sewerage, baths, and electric lights. Here are located the main office, the doctor's office, the assembly room, the dining room, the kitchen, several counselor rooms and the camp store. The entire building is screened.

Godbold Hall is the Gymnasium Recreation Hall. In one end of this building there is a thirty-foot stage, with dressing rooms on each side. On one side is a large eight-foot stone fireplace. Here on cool or rainy nights the Camp Fire program is held. The main floor of Godbold Hall is large enough for a regulation indoor basketball court or baseball diamond. The building is electrically lighted. Footlights make the staging of stunts and plays more effective.

Ten Double Cabins provide the living quarters for Jocassee girls and counselors. Each cabin accommodates ten to twelve persons, five or six to each half section. A shower bath and toilet are built in each cabin. There is also a closet for each half-section. Each cabin has a porch running the length of the front of the cabin. There is a section of screen wire running around the cabin up near the roof to provide perfect ventilation. Six of the cabins are located on the side of a hill overlooking the river, while the others are located nearer the river overlooking the lawn and Godbold Hall.

63

Hill Course

CAMP ORGANIZATION

The girls are placed in the cabins according to age and development. Ten to twelve persons will be assigned to a cabin, five or six in each section. The cabins are equipped with steel cots, with mattresses, and with mirrors. The campers are expected to bring sheets, blankets, and pillows.

The Directors strive to place each girl in a cabin according to the wishes of the girl. If a camper wishes to be placed with a special friend or group of friends, she should write the Directors before coming to camp or indicate such on her application. By doing this, much time and embarrassment can be saved. The camper that does not know any one at camp will be placed with others of the same age and development.

Indian Tribes. Each table of girls in the dining room is organized into a tribe bearing an Indian name, with counselors for leaders. Tribes are reorganized at the end of the first half term. There is a great rivalry between the tribes in song contests and on Stunt Night.

For all athletic contests the campers are divided into two groups: The Green Birds and Brown Vipers. The campers try to make their team in the different sports. Regular days are set aside for these contests. The other days are spent in instruction in the different sports.

Point System and Camp Emblem. Camp Jocassee is run on the point system. A camper earns a certain number of points for participating in each phase of camp life, and to those that make a weekly average of seven hundred and fifty points for the season of eight weeks, green and white emblems are awarded.

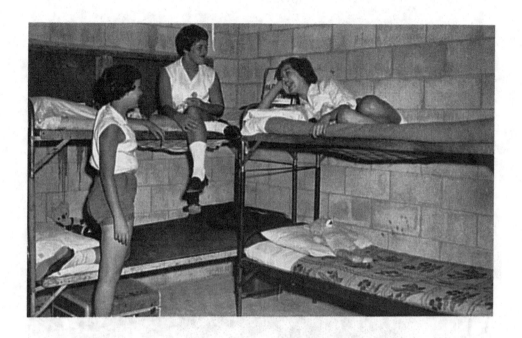

CAMP ACTIVITIES

"Setting-up" exercises are given to each camper for ten minutes at the beginning of each day. Attention is given in these exercises to correcting faulty postures. "Setting-up" is not given on Sunday nor on the mornings of long hikes.

Inspection is an important part of every day. Each girl is taught to make her bed, to straighten up her part of the cabin, to sweep and to keep her personal belongings in order.

At nine-thirty an Assembly Program is held in Godbold Hall. Here a portion of scripture is read, a short talk is made on subjects of vital interest to girls, and prayers are offered. After the announcements of the day have been made, a program of interest is offered on Monday, announcement of the weekly points is made on Tuesday, a lesson in First Aid is given on Wednesday, a program of Music or Literature Appreciation is presented on Thursday, Friday is Hiking Day, and a program of Current Events is Saturday's feature.

Every night at the close of the camp fire program counselors and campers join in singing the beautiful Jocassee evening prayer song:

"If I have wounded any soul today,
If I have caused one foot to go astray,
If I have walked in my own wilful way,
Dear Lord, forgive."

Sunday is spent in camp as a day of rest. Sunday School services are held in the morning, and occasionally a short Church service. In the afternoon the campers go for walks, a swim, and at night join in a young people's meeting.

Catholic girls have an opportunity to attend services about twice a month in Walhalla, S. C.

CAMP FIRE

"BOBBYE" FOY

If you ask any of the Jocassee campers what feature of camp life she likes best, the chances are she will answer "right off the bat"—the camp fire. There is a mystic spell cast by the camp fire that appeals to the primitive that is in everyone. It satisfies deep hidden longings of the soul.

A camp fire program features the close of every day at Camp Jocassee, and a veritable feast of soul and good fellowship it is. Singing, story-telling, impromptu shows, games, tribe parties and the like make up the program. On cool or rainy nights camp fires will be held in Godbold Hall; on fair nights, out of doors.

CAMP FIRE — GODBOLD HALL

CAMP NEWSPAPER

Under the direction of a Counselor, Jocassee campers edit a newspaper once a week. Every Tuesday night it is read at camp fire. Besides offering an opportunity for the earning of extra points, it furnishes excellent training and experience for those of a literary inclination.

TUTORING

As the requirements in the elementary and high schools become more exacting, the demands for summer schools and for coaching in the various subjects have become more urgent. Jocassee will try to furnish tutoring in almost any subject a camper may require. The time taken for this tutoring is during the part of the day that will not require the camper to miss any of the important activities of the program. The charges will be five dollars per subject per week.

DAILY PROGRAM

7:00 A.M.—Reveille.
7:10 A.M.—Setting-up.
8:00 A.M.—Breakfast.
9:15 A.M.—Inspection.
9:30 A.M.—Assembly.
10:00 A.M.—Games; Riding.
11:00 A.M.—Beginner's Swimming; Riding; Archery; Tennis.
11:30 A.M.—Diving; Advanced Swimming; Archery; Riding; Tennis.
12:30 P.M.—Life Saving; Archery; Riding; Tennis.
1:15 P.M.—Dinner.
2:00 P.M.—Quiet Hour.
3:30 P.M.—Tumbling; Dancing; Riding; Tennis.
4:00 P.M.—Tumbling; Dancing; Riding; Tennis.
4:30 P.M.—Riding; Tennis.
4:45 P.M.—Recreational Swimming.
6:00 P.M.—Supper.
7:00 P.M.—Hiking.
8:00 P.M.—Camp Fire; Songs; Stories; Stunts; Jokes; Dancing; Games.
9:00 P.M.—Retire to Cabins.
9:30 P.M.—Lights Out.
9:45 P.M.—Quiet.

Jocassee believes in regular hours, but occasionally this program is changed as the Directors and Counselors see fit.

FLAG RAISING — SHOWING RIVER CABINS

67

Tennis Courts

A part of each day is given to the instruction and playing of the most popular games for girls. Expert coaching is offered in Baseball, Kickball, Volleyball, Batball, Touchdown Passball, Hemingway Ball, Archery and Tennis. In clear weather these games are played outdoors under the lovely trees that shade the courts. In bad weather the game program is not held up, for the large gymnasium provides sufficient space for the playing of these games.

ATHLETIC

GAMES

COUNSELOR-BOOTLEG VOLLEYBALL GAME

The Tennis and Archery Tournaments each year attract a great deal of interest. Instruction is given during the season to those interested in these sports. Toward the end of the season those who wish to participate have the opportunity to take part in regulation tournaments.

HIKING

The location of Camp Jocassee affords unusual opportunities for mountain hiking, and the camp program takes full advantage of this fact. A short hike is a part of the regular daily program, and once a week a long hike is taken.

Whitewater Falls is one of the most beautiful cataracts found anywhere in the mountains. The sparkling water of the Whitewater River, as clear as an emerald, dashing over a precipice more than a hundred feet high, is beaten into a spray as white as snow. This is the favorite long hike of the Jocassee campers.

Miss Lucy Gossold
Columbia College
Columbia, S. C.

WHITEWATER FALLS

Upper Falls

Lower Falls

TIME OUT FOR LUNCH

HIKING EMBLEM

To earn this emblem a camper must do three things: Be a cheerful hiker; hike a distance of eighty miles during the season; and pass the endurance test of eight miles up hill and down without stopping.

LOVER'S LEAP HIKE — WHAT A VIEW!

WE'RE OFF!

SWIMMING AND DIVING CLASSES

All campers at Jocassee are divided into three classes for instruction work in swimming. In the first class the beginners are found working every day to learn to float and learn some one stroke. Just as soon as a beginner learns one stroke, according to standard form, she is advanced to the second class. In this class the swimmers work on additional strokes, and begin work in diving. The third class is the advanced class in diving and swimming. At times instruction and practice in Life Saving are offered in the third class.

SAFETY FIRST

No one is allowed in swimming except at the regular hours.

No one is allowed in swimming unless a life guard is on duty.

SWIMMING MEET

Every season a swimming meet is held that is open to the public. In this meet the girls compete for individual honors and team honors. Strokes for form, races, diving and so forth make up the contests. The juniors compete also. At the end of the meet, according to the points won, the champion swimmer is announced, the champion diver, and the intermediate and junior champions.

Road Trips are Popular

RIDING . . .

Horseback riding grows increasingly popular with each succeeding year at Camp Jocassee. After instruction is given on the riding field and the girls are allowed to go out on trips, the winding roads along the river banks and the trails through the mountains give a peculiar charm to this sport.

HORSE SHOW

The Horse Show is one of the most popular events at Jocassee. The campers are divided into classes according to their age and riding experience. The members of each class compete to win the blue ribbon for first place. They are judged according to their formal position, their ability to ride the different gaits and their skill in managing the horses.

Mrs. S. P. Foxgate
4204 San Amaro Drive
Coral Gables, Fla.

FAST ACTION

FUN FOR ALL!

DRAMATICS   DANCING   TUMBLING

Every Jocassee camper has an opportunity to develop whatever talent she has for dramatics. Saturday night tribe stunts, Wednesday night cabin stunts, and the final Saturday night program provide excellent training.

For dancing the girls are divided into two classes: one for beginners and one for those who have had dancing lessons before coming to Jocassee. The beginners are taught with a great deal of individual attention, and every girl is encouraged to take advantage of the dancing lessons for training in grace and body control.

Tumbling has become a very popular activity at Jocassee during the past few seasons. The fundamental rolls, head stands, hand stands, diving, balancing and pyramid building comprise most of the work of this feature.

Campers are asked to bring to camp any costumes they may have at home. They will prove quite a help in the staging of stunts, plays, and dance numbers.

Mrs. A. P. Hall
"Aunt Lucy"
Moultrie, Georgia

MEAL TIME AT JOCASSEE

Meal time at Jocassee is a happy time. Not just because the keen appetites of the campers need satisfying; not just because the meals are well planned and appetizing, but because meal time is a favorite time for singing tribe songs and the best loved camp songs. Sometimes there may be more noise than music, but always there is the note of joy and happiness.

NO BOXES OF EATABLES

We consider the health of our campers at all times; therefore we ask that no boxes of eatables of any kind be sent to campers. If they are sent, they *will not be delivered*. We hope parents and friends will not subject us to unpleasant discipline in this matter. Our camp shopper will buy fruit for the campers when it can be secured.

SUNDAY SUPPER ON THE LAWN

ANOTHER FAVORITE SPORT – ARCHERY

WHO MAY COME

Only physically sound girls of good moral character are wanted at Camp Jocassee. If a girl proves to be physically unfit for camp life, or a menace to the health of other campers, the Directors reserve the right to return her to her home. The Directors also will not hesitate to return any girl who does not submit to the discipline of the camp, or who is an obstructing factor in the discipline, without any refund of camp fees.

The Directors will not assume responsibility for an accident to a camper or a member of the staff that occurs when the camp safety rules and camp regulations are violated.

Each camper is asked to send a doctor's certificate of her physical condition before entering camp.

CAMP STORE

For the convenience of the campers a small store is opened twice a day. Here the campers may secure postals, stamps, camp paper, post cards, ink, pencils, note books, tennis balls, kodak film (when procurable), some makes of pure candy and chewing gum at regular standard prices. Camp authorities regulate the amount of candy that can be bought.

PARENT ACCOMMODATIONS

While parents are welcomed at camp and invited to watch the campers in their activities, there is no place at the camp to accommodate them. Parents are asked not to visit their daughters for the first two weeks of the season.

CAMP "DOC"

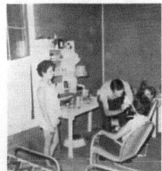

WHAT TO WEAR

Every girl at Jocassee is required to wear camp clothes at all times, but there is no set uniform.

For games, hiking and regular everyday wear there is nothing better than a dark suit of some kind, or dark shorts or slacks with white shirts or blouses.

White is the costume for Sunday. White shorts and white shirts are the favorites. White "longies" are also used.

For riding some girls use jodhpurs, some use regular riding trousers and boots, while many use blue jeans and oxfords.

When the days and nights are cold sweaters and warm slacks are necessary. Every girl should have a pair of warm dark slacks or dungarees. Light weight sweaters will be needed quite frequently.

CAMP JEMIKI FOR BOYS

Are you interested in a camp for your boy in the same county as Jocassee? Write Mr. Neild Gordon

Belmont Abbey College
Belmont, N. C.

CHRISTMAS PARTY – SANTA CLAUS COMES

WHAT TO BRING

REQUIRED:

2 Pillow cases
4 Small sheets
1 Pillow
2 Double blankets
8 Bath towels
White shorts (2 to 4 prs.)
White shirts (4 to 6)
Dark shorts (4 to 6 prs.)
Sport shirts (4 to 6)
   (Colored or T shirts)
1 Pr. black or dark blue shorts
2 Pr. dungarees or warm dark slacks
2 Light weight sweaters
1 Heavy sweater
2 Bathing suits
Riding clothes
   (Jodhpurs, blue jeans or riding pants)
Pair leather or saddle oxfords
Pair tennis shoes
Underwear

Socks
Pajamas (1 pr. warm)
Bathrobe and Slippers
Raincoat and hood or cap
2 Cakes of soap
2 Laundry bags, large size with name of camper
   on outside of bag
Drinking cup
Tooth brush
Toilet articles
Flashlight

SUGGESTIONS:

Kodak
Bible
Tennis racquet and balls
Musical instruments
Costumes for stunts
A good book to read and lend to others
Any decorations that may improve the cabins

Our Drinking Water: 6 In. Drilled Well 100 Ft. Deep

WE LIVE AND LEARN TOGETHER AT JOCASSEE!

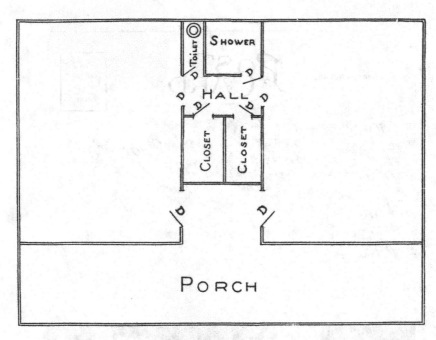

Floor Plan of Bungalows

SWIMMING MEET, CAMP JOCASSEE FOR GIRLS, JOCASSEE, S. C.

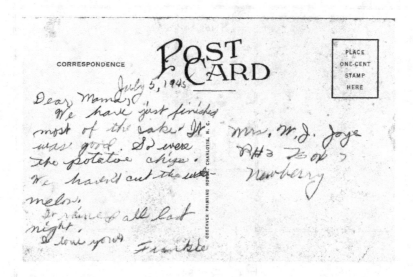

ENTRANCE GATE, CAMP JOCASSEE FOR GIRLS, JOCASSEE, S. C.

WHITEWATER RIVER, CAMP JOCASSEE FOR GIRLS, JOCASSEE, S. C.

WALLACE BUILDING, CAMP JOCASSEE FOR GIRLS, JOCASSEE, S. C.

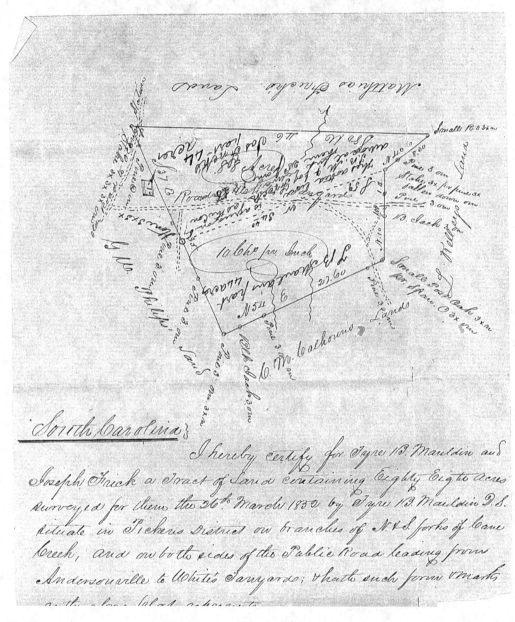

I hereby certify for Tyre B. Mauldin and Joseph Frick a Tract of Land containing Eighty Eight Acres Surveyed for them the 26th March 1852 by Tyre B. Mauldin D.S. Situate in Pickens District on branches of N & S forks of Cane Creek, And on both sides of the Public Road leading from Andersonville to White's Tanyard; & hath such form & marks

This vintage, handwritten survey is one of a number of old deeds in my collection. This one, dated 21 May 1852 and signed by W. F. Ervin, surveys 88 acres in the Pickens District on branches of N & S forks of Cane Creek.

Concerning the Browns ... and Such

Montville Justus Glazener and
Matilda Jane Whitmire Glazener

M. J. Glazener Born May 11th 1848 ⎱ Parents
Matilda J. Whitmire Born April 29th 1848 ⎰
Sarah Louise Glazener Born May 27th 1867
Giles Monroe Glazener " Dec. 23rd 1869
William Henry Glazener " Feb. 23rd 1871
Benjamin Franklin Glazener Feb 22nd 1874
Mary Malinda Glazener born April 22nd 1876
Hannie May Glazener born May 1st 1878
Clarence Bruce Glazener born Aug. 26th 1880
~~Hattie Hamilton Glazener born April 9th 18~~
Alfred Claudius Glazener Aug 26th 1883
Hattie Hamilton Glazener April 9th 1886
Norma Bell Glazener born Oct 26th 1888

William M. Brown

W. M. BROWN

W. M. Brown, 84, Passes At Home; Funeral Monday

The Keowee Courier
January 4, 1945

MR. W. M. BROWN

Oconee county has lost one of its foremost citizens in the death of Mr. W. M. Brown Saturday night. Mr. Brown was a large property owner and was in the automobile and farm supply business in Walhalla for nearly 40 years. Several years ago he was mayor and during his term many improvements were made in Walhalla, a reflection of his progressiveness. He was not content to idle away his time and continued to work until his health failed several months ago.

Mr. Brown owned considerable property in Jocassee valley, widely-known Oconee county summer resort. Vacationists and people who inhabit that area called him the "Sage of Jocassee." He invested sums and several years of his life to developing this beautiful valley.

His was an active life, and a useful one, and his memory will long be with us.

WM. M. BROWN, WALHALLA, DIES

Prominent Business, Civic, Religious Leader—Rites 2 P. M. Today

WALHALLA, Dec. 31.—William M. Brown, 84, prominent farmer and business man of Walhalla, died at his home Saturday at midnight. He was a former trustee of the then Greenville Woman's college and of Long Creek Baptist academy. For eight years he served as mayor of Walhalla.

For 40 years Mr. Brown was an active member of the Walhalla First Baptist church and contributed much to the civic, religious and business life of Walhalla and Oconee county. He was considered an outstanding champion of many worthy causes.

Before moving to Walhalla Mr. Brown owned and operated the White Water inn at Jocassee. In later years this has become Jocassee camp for girls.

Surviving are his wife, Mrs. Lou Glazener Brown; five children, Mrs. C. O. Williams, Arthur, Clyde, Lloyd and Morris Brown; one brother, N. M. Brown; 22 grandchildren and two great-grandchildren.

Funeral services will be conducted at Walhalla First Baptist church Monday at 2 p. m. by Rev. R. S. Cooper and Rev. J. H. Brown. Burial will be in West View cemetery.

Pallbearers will be G. E. Medford, Enos Abbott, Kenneth Oeaton, Freeman Bearden, Harry Earle and Glenn D. Abbott.

Honorary escort will be composed of the following who were requested to meet at the church at 1:45 p. m.: S. L. Verner, Col. R. T. Jaynes, W. J. Hunt, Hayne Jones, C. W. Pitchford, Edward Ninestein, G. J. Hunter, L. M. Brown, C. W. and J. E. Bauknight, Crayton Whitmire, T. V. Derrick, Ed Barker and Dr. G. T. Davis. Granddaughters will serve as flowerbearers. The body is at the home.

William M. Brown, 84 years of age, died at his home in Walhalla Saturday at midnight. Mr. Brown, who was a prominent farmer and business man of Walhalla, had been in declining health for the last several months.

Funeral services were conducted Monday from the Walhalla First Baptist church, conducted by the pastor, the Rev. R. S. Cooper, assisted by Dr. Edgar Morgan, of Westminster, and the Rev. J. H. Brown, pastor of St. Luke Methodist church. Interment followed in West View cemetery.

Pallbearers were G. E. Medford, Ennis Abbott, Kenneth Deaton, Freeman Bearden, Harry Earle and Glenn D. Abbott.

Honorary escort was composed of the following who were requested to meet at the church at 1:45 p. m.: S. L. Verner, Col. R. T. Jaynes, W. J. Hunt, Hayne Jones, C. W. Pitchford, Edward Ninestein, G. J. Hunter, L. M. Brown, C. W. and J. E. Bauknight, Ed Barker and Dr. J. T. Davis. Granddaughters served as flowerbearers.

Mr. Brown was a former mayor of Walhalla for eight years and during his terms many civic improvements were made. He was a high type citizen and ocntributed much to the civic, religious and business life of Walhalla and Oconee county. He was considered a champion of many worthy causes. For more than 40 years Mr. Brown was an active member of the Walhalla First Baptist church, which he served as deacon.

In addition to operating an automobile and farm supply business, Mr. Brown engaged extensively in farming. He was a former trustee of the then Greenville Woman's college and of Long Creek Baptist academy.

Before moving to Walhalla, Mr. Brown owned and operated the White Water Inn at Jocassee. In later years this became Jocessee camp for girls. Mr. Brown played a big part in developing Jocassee valley.

Surviving are his wife, Mrs. Lou Glazener Brown; five children, Mrs. C. O. Williams, Arthur Brown, Clyde Brown, Lloyd Brown, and Morris Brown; one brother, N. M. Brown; 22 grandchildren, and two great grandchildren.

Clyde C. Brown

Clyde Brown

Mr. and Mrs. W. M. Brown
Pearl Brown, wife of Clyde

Clyde Brown *august 1, 95*
WALHALLA — Clyde Calhoun Brown, 91, of 105 North Pine St., died Wednesday.

He was a retired cattleman and farmer, a veteran of World War I, and was a member of St. Luke's United Methodist Church.

Surviving are his wife, Pearl Jennings Brown of the home; and three daughters, Virginia Grobusky of Walhalla, Grace Schap of Chicago, Ill., and Ellen Alexander of Weldon, N.C.

Services: 11 a.m. Friday at the Davenport Funeral Home, Walhalla, with burial in Westview Cemetery.

Visitation: 7 to 9 p.m. Thursday at the funeral home.

In lieu of flowers, memorials may be made to St. Luke United Methodist Church.

MRS. W. B. POOLE DIES IN HOSPITAL

After Four Weeks Of Illness Mrs. Ruth Brown Poole, Daughter of Mr. and Mrs. W. M. Brown, Succumbs In Greenville—Was Interested In Singing and Music Over State.

(Greenville News.)

Mrs. Ruth Brown Poole, wife of William B. Poole, and prominent young matron of this city, died at 7 o'clock Wednesday night at a local hospital, following four weeks of illness. Mrs. Poole was born at Jocassee, a daughter of W. M. and Mrs. Lou Glazener Brown, and moved to Walhalla with her parents in young girlhood. She completed high school there, after which she matriculated at Greenville Woman's College, where she specialized in music and obtained her degree.

Mrs. Poole took an interest in the Greenville Music Club, being a past president. She served as a member of the executive board of the State Federation of Music Clubs. She also served for four or five years as State chairman of the Atwater-Kent auditions for the State and was appointed as one of the judges in one of these events. At the time of her death, she was soprano soloist at Christ Episcopal Church.

Mrs. Poole was a member of the Greenville Country Club, and of Buncombe Street Methodist Episcopal Church, where for a number of years she was a member of the choir.

Mr. Poole is associated with the Ballenger Paving Company, and he survives her ,together with two little daughters, Blanche Poole, 11, and Ruth Poole, 9.

Her parents, Mr. and Mrs. W. M. Brown, of Walhalla, also survive, as does one sister, Mrs. Myrtle B. Williams, of Columbia, and the following brothers: Arthur, Clyde and Morris Brown, all of Walhalla, and Lloyd Brown, of Seneca.

Funeral services were held Friday afternoon at 4 o'clock at the Mackey Mortuary, conducted by Dr. B. R. Turnipseed and Rev. Robt. T. Phillip. Interment was in Springwood cemetery.

The many Walhalla friends of the family join with The Courier in extending sympathy to them in their bereavement.

MRS. WILLIAM POOLE, past president of the Greenville Music club and a delegate to the State Federation of Music clubs to Spartanburg and one of Greenville's most popular sopranos, possessing a lovely voice of much sweetness. She has been soprano leader in several of the largest choirs of the city and assisted at many musical affairs.

MRS W. B. POOLE BE LAID TO REST

Services At 4 This Afternoon For Prominent Local Resident

Funeral services for Mrs. Ruth Brown Poole, resident of 415 West Prentiss avenue, who died at a local hospital at 7 o'clock Wednesday evening, will be held this afternoon at 4 o'clock, at the Mackey mortuary. The services will be conducted by Dr. B. Rhett Turnipseed and the Rev. Robert T. Phillips, and the interment will be made in Springwood cemetery.

The following persons will serve as the active pallbearers: Donald J. Bull, Emory N. Smith, F. D. Meadors, John Bateman, John D. Smeak, J. J. McKinzie, Joe A. Garrett and C. R. McDonald.

Those composing the honory escort are: Dr. F. Jordan, Dr. E. W. Carpenter, Dr. T. B. Reeves, Dr. J. W. Boggs, L. P. Hollis, George Schaefer, Dr. David M. Ramsey, C. P. Ballenger, J. Will Hunter, B. H. Martin, John W. Arrington, Jr., M. L. Marchant, R. Torrence, Arthur Merritt, Belton O'Neall and Dr. B. S. Allen.

Mrs. Poole was a daughter of W. M. Brown and Mrs Lou Glazener Brown and was reared at Jocasse, where she finished high school, later attending Greenville Woman's college, from which institution she was graduated with a degree in music. Mrs. Poole possessed an unusual soprano voice and was an enthusiastic member of the Greenville music club, which organization she had served as president. She served on the executive board of the State Federation of Music, and as state chairman of the Atwater-Kent auditions in this state for four or five consecutive years. She also

had the honor of serving as judge in these events. At the time of her death she was soprano soloist at Christ Episcopal church, and in former years was a member of the choir of the Buncombe Street Methodist Episcopal church, of which church she was a member. Mrs. Pool was also a member of the Greenville Country club.

She is survived by her husband, William B. Poole, and by two little daughters, Blanche Poole, 11, and Ruth Poole, 9. Her parents, Mr. and Mrs. W. M. Brown, of Walhalla, also survive, and one sister, Mrs. Myrtle B. Williams, of Columbia, and the following brothers: Arthur Brown, Clyde Brown and Morris Brown, all of Walhalla, and Lloyd Brown, of Seneca.

Until the hour of the services, the body will remain at the Mackey mortuary.

Blanche Poole Mann

*William B. Poole and daughter,
Blanche*

Miss Blanche Poole United With Ensign Mann—Rites In Alexandria, Va. March 11

Of unusual interest is the marriage of Miss Blanche Poole and Fletcher Cullen Mann, Ensign, United States Naval Reserve, which took place in Alexandria, Va., on March 11. The vows were spoken at 2 o'clock in the afternoon at St. Paul's Episcopal church, with Rev. Stanley Brown Serman officiating.

Miss Ruth Poole of this city, only sister of the bride, was maid of honor, She wore a street dress of aqua, with white flower hat, white gloves and other accessories in black. Her corsage was of gardenias.

Ensign Mann was attended by his uncle, Richard Outlaw, of Washington, as best man.

The bride, who was given in marriage by her father, William B. Poole, of this city, wore a street length dress in shell pink, with matching flowered half-hat and veil. Her accessories were in navy blue. Her only ornament was a strand of pearls, a gift of the bridegroom. She carried a bouquet of white freesias and sweet peas centered with a purple orchid.

Mrs. Mann is the daughter of William B. Poole and the late Mrs. Ruth Brown Poole of Greenville. Her maternal grandparents are Mr. and Mrs. W. M. Brown of Walhalla and her paternal grandparents are E. S. Poole and the late Mrs. Poole. She attended the schools of this city and is now a senior at the Woman college of the University of North Carolina, in Greensboro where she plans to return to graduate.

Ensign Mann is the son of Mrs. Fletcher Mann, formerly of Pittsboro, N. C., now of Washington, and the late Mr. Mann. He was graduated from the University of North Carolina where he was president of the Young Democrats club. He did post graduate work at George Washington university and prior to entering service held a position with the Department of Agriculture in Washington.

For traveling, the bride changed to a suit in navy with matching hat and wore as corsage the orchid from her bouquet.

Those attending the wedding from this city included the bride's parents, Mr. and Mrs. W. B. Poole, and her sister, Miss Ruth Poole.

MRS. MANN
(Photo by Princeton)

Ruth Poole Boyd

MRS. CHARLES THOMAS BOYD, JR., who last evening became the bride of Major Boyd, was Miss Ruth Poole, daughter of Mr. and Mrs. William B. Poole. The nuptials were solemnized at Buncombe Street Methodist church.

MISS RUTH POOLE IS BRIDE OF MAJOR BOYD IN CHURCH CEREMONY

Miss Ruth Poole was united in marriage with Maj. Charles Thomas Boyd, Jr., of Jacksonville, Fla., in a wedding held Saturday evening, February 23 at eight-thirty o'clock in Buncombe street Methodist church with Rev. John Owen Smith officiating.

The service was held by candle light in a setting of white blossoms against a background of bamboo and palms. Mrs. Dudley Withers at the organ, furnished the wedding music.

Serving as ushers were Capt. Clark Bartlett, Lt. Fletcher C. Mann, brother-in-law of the bride, Lt. Fred Swindel, Lt. Col. Harry Fromme of Jacksonville, Fla., and Capt. James C. Lanier, Jr.

The bride was attended by her sister, Mrs. Fletcher C. Mann, as matron of honor. Maids were the Misses Virginia and Mary Ewing Boyd, sisters of the bridegroom, Miss Frances Stevenson of Columbia, Miss Shirley Morris of Greenville and Miss Billie Burns of Lancaster. They wore dresses of light blue marquisette fashioned alike with round yoke, fitted bodice, cap sleeves and full skirt. Their gloves and headdresses matched their dresses in color and they carried bouquets of Dutch iris and King Alfred jonquils.

The bride, who was given in marriage by her father, wore a gown of ivory brocaded satin with drop shoulders and a yoke of satin marquisette. The fitted bodice was pointed front and back and was fastened down the back with self-covered buttons. The long sleeves ended in points over the wrists. Her fingertip veil was attached to a Mary Queen of Scots deaddress and she carried a boquet of calla lilies.

Lt. Robert I. Travis of Jacksonville, Fla., attened the bridegroom as best-man.

Following the ceremony, a reception was held at the Poinsett hotel for out of town guests.

Later the couple left for a wedding trip to New York. For travel, the bride wore an olive green gabardine suit with matching hat and black accessories topped with a black tuxedo coat trimmed with silver fox fur.

Mrs. Boyd is the daughter of Mr. and Mrs. William Bass Poole of this city. She is a graduate of Sullins school, Bristol, Va., and of Furman university. She is a past president of the Junior Cotillion.

Maj. Boyd is the son of Mrs. Charles Thomas Boyd and the late Mr. Boyd. Before entering the army in March, 1941 he was a law student at the University of Florida. He served 37 months overseas in Newfoundland, Australia, India and China. At present he is stationed with headquarters of the Army air forces at Washington.

The couple will reside at Washington until April when Maj. Boyd will receive a discharge from the air forces and resume his study of law at the University of Florida.

Out-of-town guests at the wedding included Miss Joan Myers of White Plains, N. Y.; Mrs. C. O. Williams of Columbia; Miss Ruth Maddox of Atlanta, Ga.; Mr. and Mrs. Sidney Braswell of Birmingham, Ala.; Mrs. W. M. Brown of Walhalla and Miss Kathleen Ward of Edenton, N. C.

M. Hunter Brown
George Prince Brown
Lloyd Brown
Morris & Lucy Brown

Morris and Lucy Brown

M. Hunter Brown

WALHALLA — M. Hunter Brown, 43, of 210 Holloway St., died in Atlanta, Ga., Saturday.

Born in Oconee County, son of Mrs. Lucy Hunter Brown of Walhalla and the late Morris E. Brown, he was a past president of Walhalla Jaycees, had received Key Man awards and distinguished service awards as chairman of Parks and Recreation Committee for Walhalla, was a clerk at Walhalla Post Office and had served in the U.S. Army, and was a member of St. John Lutheran Church, where he was treasurer.

Surviving also are his wife, Mrs. Betty Addis Brown; two sons, Louis and Allen Brown of the home; two daughters, Misses Carol and Cathy Brown of the home; one brother, Paul Brown of Walhalla; and two sisters, Mrs. Julia Ballenger of Westminster and Mrs. Caroline Williams of Newport News, Va.

Funeral services will be at 4 p.m. Monday at St. John Lutheran Church, with burial in the church cemetery.

The body is at Davenport Funeral Home where the family

June 3, 1992

will receive friends from 7 to 9 p.m. Sunday.

Memorials may be made to St. John Church building fund.

The body will be placed in the church at 3 p.m. Monday.

Lloyd Brown

SENECA — Lloyd Brown, 67, livestock dealer, died Wednesday at Veterans Hospital in Columbia.

Mr. Brown was the brother of the late Mrs. Osborne Williams of Columbia.

Survivors include his widow, the former Wyllie Davis of the home; three daughters, Mrs. Mitylene Irick of Bowling Green, Ky., Mrs. Bootsie Richardson of Seneca and Mrs. Lillis Smith of Charlotte, N. C., and two brothers, Arthur and Clyde Brown of Walhalla.

Graveside services will be held at 5 p.m. Friday in Oconee Memorial Park near Seneca.

The body is at the Seneca Mortuary.

George Prince Brown

WALHALLA — George Prince Brown, 46, of 306 N. Church St., died Monday in Anderson.

He was born in Oconee County, son of Arthur Brown of Walhalla and the late Mrs. Grace Prince Brown, was a World War II veteran, member of Blue Ridge Masonic Lodge and St. Luke's Methodist Church.

Surviving also are his wife, Mrs. Ruth Moore Brown; two sons, George Prince Brown Jr. and Charles Rodney Brown of the home; a daughter, Miss June Brown of the home; a brother, Eugene Brown of Walhalla; three sisters, Miss Elva Brown and Mrs. Rose Cashin of Walhalla and Mrs. Jo Ann Summey of Mauldin; and his stepmother, Mrs. Glenda C. Brown of Walhalla.

Graveside services will be Tuesday at 2 p.m. in West View Cemetery.

Grace Brown

Grace Brown

Tribute to Grace Brown.

In loving remembrance of Grace Brown, by Young People's Missionary Society of the Walhalla Methodist church.

In the early dawn of the morning of May 25th, 1920, the death angel hovered over the bed and clasped to its bosom the beautiful soul of Grace Brown and bore it on wings of love to its heavenly home.

For more than three months this brave girl fought desperately to gain back her strength and health, which was destroyed so utterly from the effects of influenza. She was always smiling and always cheerful, and ever thoughtful of the loved ones who ministered to her needs. So bright and witty at times was this sweet girl that it was hard to believe that her illness was so serious, and to a large degree it was not realized even by those nearest and dearest to her.

But surely and slowly, it seemed, the dread malady held firmly on, the heart grew weaker and weaker, the blood continued its waste until, in a desperate moment, the loved physician who had labored so patiently and called forth all his best skill to check the dread malady, decided on the last hope. So, on Sunday afternoon, May the 23d, Grace was carried to Baltimore in a vain hope that the skilled specialists might be able to prolong the life of this dear girl. All the way on this long journey this brave girl was desperately ill, and her chance for relief grew slimmer and slimmer. Soon after reaching Baltimore the great specialists realized their skill was in vain. Every effort proved futile. So in the early dawn, as Nature was awakening from her drowsiness, as the birds began to sing their glad song of a new day, this brave, sweet girl closed her eyes in a deep slumber and awoke "over on the other shore," where there will be no more suffering, no more partings, but there Grace will await the coming of all those she loved in this life.

In the death of Grace the Missionary Society loses a valuable member—one who, at every call, responded to duty with a willingness and a resolve to do her best "in the dear Lord's work."

Grace was present at the last meeting of the society in April, and, though she was extremely weak, her sweet voice rose in tremulous tones to "Rock of Ages, Cleft for me."

The urgent need of the whole world had so impressed this lovely girl that she had expressed a desire to become a missionary. But Grace's mission had been fulfilled; and, although her young life came to a close so early—for she was just 14 years of age—she had gladdened many a heart, and her precious influences are left to guide many to the throne of Jesus.

Long will the memory of his sweet girl linger in the hearts of the members of the society.

Truck Overturns, Columbian Killed

CLINTON, May 28.—Mrs. Coleman O. Williams, 54, 439 Deerwood Dr., Columbia, was killed on the outskirts of the city limits today when she fell out of a truck that later overturned and crushed her.

Her husband, who was driving a 1947 Dodge pickup truck, said his wife fell out of the right hand door. A trailer was being pulled.

Mr. Williams said the right rear tire blew out as the two were on their way to their summer cottage at Jocessee. Mrs. Williams had returned Saturday from a visit to her son, Maj. C. O. Williams Jr., in Hawaii.

Sheriff C. W. Wier of Laurens County quoted investigating officers as believing the trailer had something to do with causing the truck to overturn. Mr. Williams said he was driving about 35 miles an hour. The accident occurred about 500 feet from the southeast city limits on Highway 76. The truck turned over on its right side and was but slightly damaged.

Mr. Williams a Southern Railway conductor, was uninjured but a small dog in the truck was also killed.

Mrs. Williams was the former Miss Myrtle Brown. Survivors include her husband; a daughter, Mrs. James B. Richardson, Greensboro, N. C.; two sons, Major Williams, Hickam Field, Hawaii, and Frederick B. Williams, a student at The Citadel.

The body was taken to the Gray Funeral Home here and then to the Dunbar Funeral Home in Columbia.

Cpl. H. L. Patrick of the State Highway Patrol and Deputies H. R. Jones and Paul Prince of Sheriff Wier's force investigated.

Elva Brown
Myrtle Brown Williams
C. Osborne "Buck" Williams
Betty Lutrelle Williams Richardson
Frederick Brown Williams
Mr. & Mrs. W. M. Brown
Blanche Poole Mann
Ruth Poole Boyd
Bootsie Brown Richardson
Louise Brown

Miss Betty Williams, dauhgter of Mr. and Mrs. C. O. Williams, will return home today from Seneca, where she has been the guest of her cousin, Miss Louise Brown, the past three weeks.

GREENVILLE VISITORS

Mrs. C. O. Williams has had as her guests for the past few days, her nieces, Misses Blanche and Ruth Poole of Greenville. Blanche will be a junior at the University of North Carolina, woman's division, Greensboro. N. C., this year, and Ruth will be a freshman at Furman university, Greenville.

—Miss Elva Brown has as her guest for two weeks Miss Josephine Tomlinson, of High Point, N. C.

—Mrs. C. O Williams, Osborne, Betty and Frederic Wiliams have returned to their home in Columbia after spending the past month as the guests of Mrs. Williams' parents, Mr. and Mrs. W. M. Brown.

—Misses Blanche a n d Ruth Poole, of Greenville, and Miss Bootsie Brown, of Seneca, were recent visitors to their grandparents, Mr. and Mrs. W. M. Brown.

—Little Martha Joyce Morse, daughter of Mr .and Mrs. Elbert Morse, is visiting he grandmother, Mrs. D. M. Watson, in Anderson, this week.

Miss Louise Brown of Seneca, who has been visiting her aunt, Mrs. C. O. Williams, in Columbia for several weeks, has returned to her home. She was accompanied by her cousin, Miss Betty Williams. who will be away several weeks. Miss Williams will visit her cousins, Misses Blanche and Ruth Poole, in Greenville before returning to Columbia.

Lou Brown with children (l to r)
Ruth, Grace, Morris, Myrtle

(l to r) Pop, Fred, Buck, Myrtle, Jim, Jimmy

Aunts and Cousins gather on the steps in front of Attakulla Lodge

Fred (center) at The Citadel

Buck

Top (l to r): Ruth Brown, Unidentified, Myrtle Brown
Middle (l to r): Matilda Glazener, Lou Brown, Unidentified
Bottom (l to r): Grace Brown, Morris Brown

Generations in Whitewater River

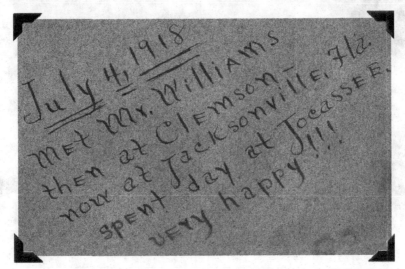

July 4, 1918
Met Mr. Williams
then at Clemson—
now at Jacksonville, Fla.
spent day, at Jocassee.
very happy !!!!

An entry in Myrtle's scrapbook

101

Myrtle and Buck (or Betty)

My brother, Jimmy, in a bateau

Myrtle

Myrtle and Fred swim in front of the Lodge

Pop, Jimmy, Myrtle, and friends

while Wayne McCoy takes a creature approach

Betty wades in front of the Lodge

Mother cools off, while Wayne McCall takes a creative approach!

Melanie and Debbie, on inner tubes - what else!

Debbie and Melanie - our favorite place through the years

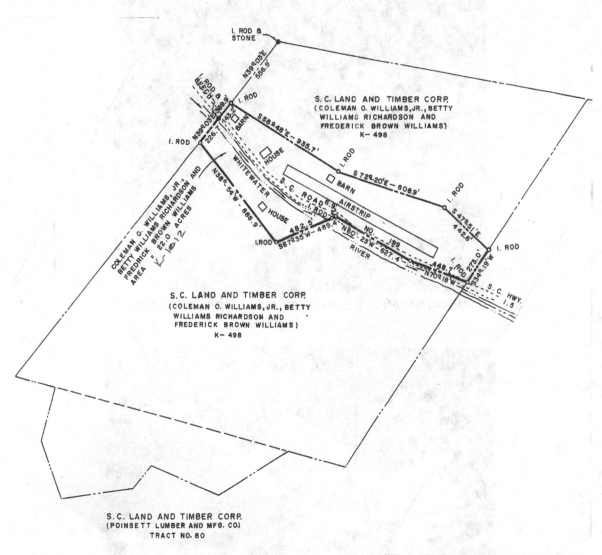

This is the survey of my family's Jocassee property, totaling 276 acres. The bottom 22 acres was the valley portion where the houses and airstrip were situated. Only recently did I find out that the property reached out so far in both directions that . . . we ALMOST had lakefront property when Lake Jocassee was at full pond. According to the plat (which I also have a copy of superimposed on the lake map), our property went a considerable distance up Double Springs and McKinney's Mountains. This is the actual survey that will be used to determine the GPS coordinates to aid in our search for Attakulla Lodge.

Bridges of Oconee County

Mother sunning herself on the swinging bridge, Summer of 1945
(my favorite picture of her)

Chapman's Bridge
(The posted sign announces an upcoming REVIVAL!)

Cousin Becky . . . a little shallow for diving,
I think!

Chapman's Bridge spans the Keowee River
(Both photos courtesy Duke Power Archives)

Chapman's Bridge in its new location on Lake Keowee.
Unfortunately, it was destroyed by arsonists.

This is the coffer dam which is at the present site of Devil's Fork State Park. This view, taken from the swimming area, shows Press Holcombe's old house, which has now been replaced by the ranger station and gift shop. Pop and Exie built a home up the road from here when they vacated Attakulla Lodge.
(Courtesy Duke Power Archives)

A River Ran Through It

Beautiful Whitewater River - the lifeblood of Jocassee Valley

Looking upriver

Rapids racing to the swimming hole

A peaceful calm

If you look closely, you can see a swimmer standing at the swimming hole.

Mirrored images

The swimming hole (also known as the Baptizing Hole)
as photographed from Miss Sarah's bluff
(Courtesy of Anna Simon)

1945

1960's

From the steel bridge, looking downstream in the direction of the present-day site of the dam

A little further upriver

Circa 1920's

Fly fishing on the shoals underneath the steel bridge

Murder!

News about Jocassee Valley and its residents was not always peaceful. In 1931, the *Keowee Courier* reported the murder of C. Fred Brown.

(original paper and photographs reproduced; article transcribed for readability)

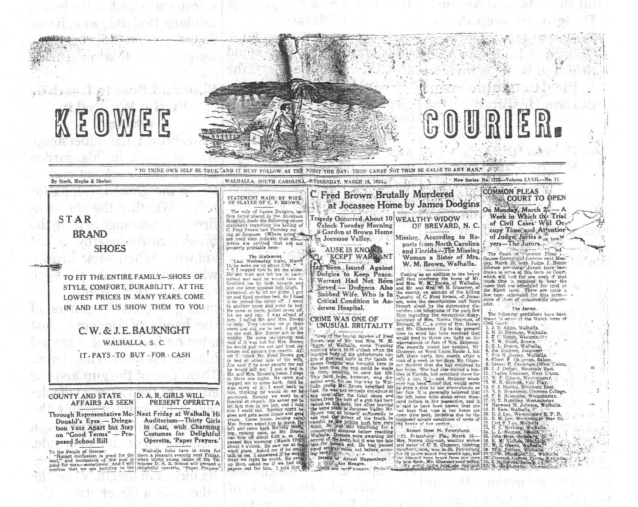

C. Fred Brown Brutally Murdered at Jocassee Home by James Dodgins

Tragedy Occurred About 10 O'clock Tuesday Morning In Garden at Brown Home in Jocassee Valley.

NO CAUSE IS KNOWN EXCEPT WARRANT

Had Been Issued Against Dodgins to Keep Peace. Warrant Had Not Been Served — Dodgons Also Stabbed Wife, Who is In Critical Condition in Anderson Hospital.

CRIME WAS ONE OF UNUSUAL BRUTALITY

News of the brutal murder of Fred Brown, son of Mr. and Mrs. W. M. Brown, of Walhalla, came Tuesday morning about 10:30 o'clock when the mangled body of the unfortunate victim of gun and knife in the hands of James Dodgins was brought here in the hope that the trip could be made in time, possibly, to save his life. This faint hope, however, was dispelled soon, for on the way to Walhalla young Mr. Brown breathed his last. He was not entirely conscious at any time after the fatal shots and blows from the butt of a gun had been rained on his body, but after leaving the home place in Jocassee Valley Mr. Brown was at himself sufficiently to ask that the driver of the truck be careful, as the jolting hurt him very much. He was still breathing for a considerable distance before reaching Walhalla. Doctors were awaiting the arrival of the body, but it was too late late for human aid. He had passed away several miles out before arriving here.

Details of Actual Happenings Are Meagre

Details are very meagure. Probably the one who could give the most help on the matter, Mrs. Fred Brown, is in a highly nervous state, nearing breakdown, and nobody has questioned her minutely. It was she, however, who wrested the gun from the hands of Dodgins after her husband had been shot and after two savage blows had been dealt over the head of the suffering victim.

Peace Warrant Obtained Monday Afternoon.

Mr. and Mrs. Brown accompanied Mrs. Dodgins, wife of the slayer, to Walhalla Monday afternoon, and after legal advice in the situation, a warrant was issued to be served on Dodgins to keep the peace.

The warrant was never served. As Officer P. S. Shook, accompanied by Magistrate Burt Gillespie and Clerk of Court G. W. Shirley, went up toward Jocassee to serve the warrant they met the truck carrying the body of Mr. Brown, and a car coming along with that party, in which were a special deputy and Dodgins, he having been placed under arrest and was on the way to jail. It was understood, we are told, that Mr. Shook was to go up Monday afternoon to make the arrest, but for some reason he did not get off that evening. Mr. and Mrs. Brown and the wife of Dodgins, it is said, felt safe in going back to the home, thinking Dodgins, who, it was feared, might kill his wife, would be in safe keeping of the law.

Shot and Beat to Death as Victim Worked in Garden.

Mr. Brown, it is understood, was at work in his garden when a shot rang out and he fell to the ground, calling for help. Whether the shot was fired at close range or from the brush growth nearby is not known. When Mrs. Brown, who was not at all well, reached the scene, she managed to get the gun out of the hands of Dodgins just after he had struck a second blow on the head of his victim. Then, free of the gun and the efforts of the victim's wife, he pulled his knife, slashing the throat on one side and giving a vicious stab on the other side. The one blow cut a gash about six inches in length, while the other was a direct stab. The jugular vein was not severed, however, and the stab wound being about two inches deep, ending when the knife blade struck the neck bone.

The gunshot wound and one of the blows from the butt of the gun were sufficient to have either caused death. One side of the head was laid bare to the bone, but the skull was not crushed. The other blow, however, crushed the skull and it was shattered like an eggshell. The marvel is that the young man clung to life at all after the shot and the blows. Examination of some of the missiles that entered the body of Mr. Brown indicate that the shells had been loaded with some kind of slugs. There were some objects that looked like small buckshot, and others were reported to be almost square and jagged. The main load entered the body just above the hip and came out through the pit of the stomach, showing that, from whatever point the shot was fired, it was fired from the back. It is not definitely known, but it is possible that two shots were fired at him. Some shot were about the shoulder, and a jagged stroke as of some irregular object furrowed its way along one arm, rending it with a deep gash-like wound.

Mr. Brown was born in Transylvania County, North Carolina, 40 years ago. When he was a small child his parents moved to Jocassee. At the time of his death he was engaged in farming. Dodgins, the man who killed him, and his wife, lived in a part of the Brown home, Dodgins being in the employ of Mr. Brown. Recently Mrs. Dodgins came over to the portion of the house occupied by the Browns and requested that she be permitted to stay there as a protection from her husband. It is said by some that the latter had been drinking a great deal of late.

(After reading the statement made by the wife of James Dodgins, we find that there are some minor inaccuracies in our account of the killing as we gathered it from what statements . . .).

STATEMENT MADE BY WIFE OF SLAYER OF C. F. BROWN

The wife of James Dodgins, before being placed in the Anderson Hospital, made the following sworn statement regarding the killing of C. Fred Brown last Tuesday morning at Jocassee. (Where asterisks are used they indicate that statements are omitted that are not properly printable here:

The Statement.

"Last Wednesday night, March 11, he woke me up about 1:30. * * * * I begged him to let me alone. He got mad and hit me in back; cursed and said he would take it. Grabbed me by both breasts and put one knee against left thigh. I screamed, so he let me alone. I got up and fixed another bed. As I fixed it he jerked the cover off. I went to another room and went to bed. He came in there, pulled cover off, hit me and ran. I was afraid of him. I called Mr. and Mrs. Brown to help. They carried me in their room and put me to bed. I got in on one side, Mrs. Brown got in the middle. He came in cursing and said if it was not for Mrs. Brown he would pull me out and bust my brains out against the hearth. After 3 o'clock Mr. Fred Brown got in bed on other side of his wife. Jim said if he ever caught me out he would kill me. I put a bed in Mr. and Mrs. Brown's room. I slept in there one night. He came and begged me to come back. Said he was sorry of it. I went back to him, thinking he would do as he promised. Sunday we went to a funeral at church. He asked me to let him ride in my lap, and I told him I could not. Sunday night he goes and gets some liquor and gets drunk. Came home, raising cain. Mrs. Brown asked him to leave. He left and came back Monday morning, raising cane, so Mr. Brown ran him off about 8:30 a.m. He passed this morning (March 17th) about 8 o'clock. He saw me at the wash place. Asked me if he could talk to me. I answered if he would treat me right he could. He came up then, asked me if we had any papers out for him. I told him I had a peace warrant. He said he was going to the store. He left and came back about 10 o'clock. Mrs. Brown wanted some mustard seed sowed. Asked me if I would help Mr. Brown sow them, as she was in bed sick. I went, and as we got the seed sowed, we heard a gun fire. Some of the shot hit me and Mr. Brown. We saw we were too far from the house to run. We ran down the road behind a high bank, so he shot again, and some shot hit me again. About that time we thought we could get to the house. By the time we made a few steps he was right at us. He shot Mr. Brown and he fell. Then he ran at me to hit me with his gun on my head. I threw my left arm up and he hit me on my left arm. He then turned back on Mr. Brown and took his knife to him. I thought I could get to the house, and started. He overtook me and caught me by my collar, and said, "Come on; I am going to finish you up." I begged him to stop, but he cursed me; said he didn't care; he hit me and then knocked me down with his gun, and after I was down he hit me again and drug me about 30 feet by my feet. Took his knife; kept trying to get to my throat. I kept my arm up so he could not get to my throat. He stabbed me in my left breast; kept on pressing the knife deeper. Finally he left and said he was going back to old Brown and finish him up if he was not dead. While he was gone I tried to stagger to the house. He trailed by the blood and found me and pulled me out of the closet. Said he was going to finish killing me. I begged so hard he said he would let me alone. Said he thought I would die anyway.

Wherever I speak of "he" and "him" I have reference to Jimmy Dodgens.

(Signed) Etta Dodgins.

Sworn to this March 17, 1931,

G. W. Shirley. C.C.P.
Witness: James S. Wilson.

Slashes Wife, Who May Die

There was no one about the premises to hinder the apparently blood-crazed man, and he found his wife and stabbed her in the breast, inflicting a very painful and possibly fatal wound. She was taken to the Anderson Hospital, where it was said that no statement could at the time be made as to her recovery. She was suffering from frequent coughing spells, and at each of these attacks the blood was forced through the wound in her breast. She is about 30 or 35 years of age, and her husband is about the same age. Besides the serious breast wound she is suffering from numerous wounds in the head and about the body, inflicted by her husband with the butt of the gun. Physicians figure her chances of recovery about 75%, unless unforeseen complication arise. The gun was in possession this morning of Sheriff Thomas. It is a single barrel back loading gun, broken clean at the stock by the force of the blows struck by the murderer. Three shots were fired by Didgins, according to a statement by Deputy Tom Massey, who said that Dodgins made this statement in his presence. Dodgins had three shells, he said — two loaded with small shot and one with buckshot. Dodgins made no mention of a slug-loaded shell. This may have been only conjecture on the part of those who examined the many-shaped objects taken from the wounds on Mr. Brown's body.

Funeral to Be Held Today.

Funeral services will be held this afternoon at 4 o'clock from the residence of Mr. and Mrs. W. M. Brown, his parents. The interment will be made in West View cemetery.

The sad death of Mr. Brown is very greatly deplored on all sides, and the sympathy of all goes out to the bereaved ones.

The deceased is survived by his parents, Mr. and Mrs. W. M. Brown, of Walhalla, and four brothers — Arthur, Clyde, Lloyd and Morris Brown, also of Walhalla; and by two sisters, Mrs. C. O. Williams, of Columbia, and Mrs. Wm. B. Poole, of Greenville.

He was twice married, his first wife having been Miss Nora Beattie, of the Picket Post section of Oconee. One son, William Brown, a child by first marriage, also survives him. His second wife was Miss Ione Boggs, of Pickens, who survives him.

Report from Brevard, N. C.

Brevard, N. C., March 16. — The mysterious disappearance of Mrs. Norma Shipman, 40-year-old wealthy widow, two weeks ago, and the subsequent disappearance of a youth who roomed at her home, led officers to make a search for them today.

Sheriff Ed. Patton said Mrs. Shipman's home had been rifled of valuables, and a bloody sack had been discovered. He ordered the search for her and for Joe Bradley, 21, who had been associated with her in business, and had lived at her home.

Patton said he learned Mrs. Shipman had not been seen since March 11, when, in company with Bradley and a 20-year-old youth known only as "Happy" Brown, she visited a brother, Henry Glazener, of near West Union. Bradley and Brown returned here, according to Patton, and told friends of Mrs. Shipman that she had gone to visit C. B. Glazener, of St. Petersburg, Fla., a brother. Patton said he had communicated with the Florida resident and had been told that she had not been there.

The two youths were reported by neighbors to have left Brevard March 8th in two automobiles belonging to Mrs. Shipman.

Patton said he understood that Mrs. Shipman had had $7,000 in cash in her home. Mrs. Shipman is the widow of the late G. W. Shipman, sheriff of Transylvania County.

Patton said he had sent the sack to Raleigh for an analysis of the stains which he believes to be blood.

One report indicated Mrs. Shipman might have been here March 8th. It came from a group of Six-Mile, S. C., residents, who were here Saturday looking for Mrs. Shipman. The members of the party — E. G. Durham, Mrs. Irene Durham, Miss Adfield Brown and Edwin Stewart — came to the Shipman home Saturday and were questioned by officers. They said they had been here the previous Sunday and had seen Mrs. Shipman.

I found this photo of Fred Brown in Myrtle's scrapbook. The date was not specifically noted, but other photos on the same page were dated 1919. Born in 1890, he would be about 29 - approximately 22 years before his death.

DODGINS FOUND GUILTY MURDER; LIFE SENTENCE

Jury Returns Verdict at 3:15

WALHALLA, (Friday A. M., July 10.—"Guilty, with recommendation to the mercy of the court," was the verdict of the jury in the Dodgins case returned at 3:15 o'clock this morning after being out for more than 15 hours. The sentence automatically carries with it a sentence of a life imprisonment.

(Special to the Independent.)
WALHALLA, (Friday) July 10.— A mistrial loomed this morning in the case of Jim Dodgins, Oconee farmer charged with shooting to death Fred Brown, his employer, as the jury had failed to reach an agreement after deliberating for more than 12 hours.

Trial of the case was begun Monday morning. Arguments were completed at noon yesterday. Judge G. B. Greene, presiding, took approximately 30 minutes to deliver his charge. The jury retired at 12:30 o'clock and was still out at an early hour this morning.

The killing occurred at the Jocassee camp last April. Dodgins is alleged to have shot Brown in the back and to have attacked Mrs. Dodgins, wounding her severely.

A number of defense witnesses testified that the defendant was subject to epileptic fits and that he might have been in the throes of a "spell" when he killed Brown.

Testifying in his own defense, Dodgins told the court that his wife and Brown had been intimate and that when he approached Brown about the matter Brown drew a knife and avdanced on him. He then fired in self defense, Dodgins testified.

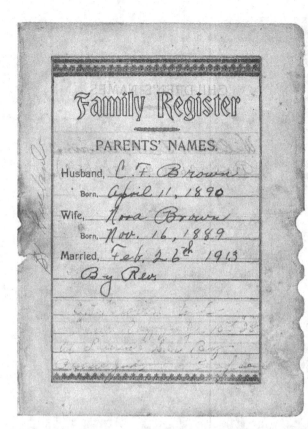

Family Register

PARENTS' NAMES.

Husband, C. F. Brown
   Born, April 11, 1890
Wife, Nora Brown
   Born, Nov. 16, 1889
Married, Feb. 26th 1913
   By Rev.

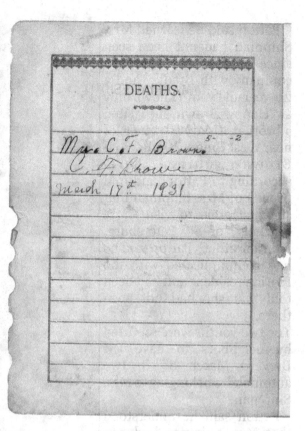

DEATHS.

Mrs. C. F. Brown.
C. F. Brown
March 17th 1931

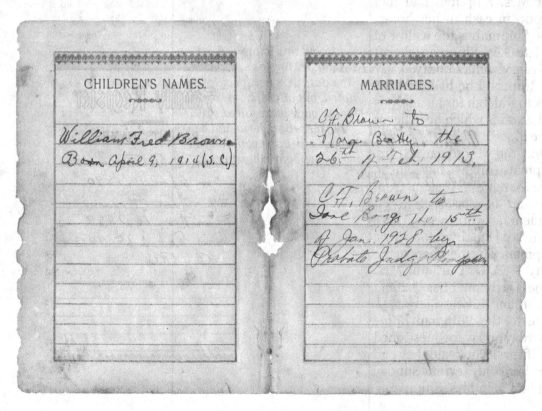

CHILDREN'S NAMES.

William Fred Brown.
Born April 9, 1914 (S. C.)

MARRIAGES.

C. F. Brown to
Nora Beatty the
26th of Feb. 1913.

C. F. Brown to
Jane Boggs the 15th
of Jan. 1938 by
Probate Judge Simpson

Shortia: A Long-Lost Treasure Found

The creation of the dam destroyed so many things – including a rare plant known as Shortia.

Keowee Courier – Thursday, September 18, 1941
(original photographs reproduced; captions and article transcribed for readability;
original – and often incorrect – spellings maintained)

Long-Lost Alpine Plant Found In Abundance in Jocassee Valley

(By Nell Flinn Gilland)

(The following account of Jocassee Valley in northeast Oconee county appeared recently in the Charlotte Observer. The cuts were furnished the Courier through the courtesy of the Observer and the Easley Progress.)

In South Carolina's alpine region, guarded by the mountains of Oconee county, lies a jewel of a valley. About 1,200 feet above sea level, it is called Jocassee, a name almost as musical as Whitewater river, which sparkles and dashes along between its verdant banks the seven miles of the valley's length. At the head of the vale are the White river waterfalls, where the stream plunges over the side of Five Mile mountain in a foaming cascade of greater height than Niagara.

Whitewater is a tributary of the Keowee. The Indian names in Oconee county are a reminder that this section was once Cherokee land. One of their towns, probably in the valley referred to, was Jocassee. An Indian legend hangs around the name, which is said to mean "The Land of the Lost One."

Legend of Jocassee

According to Mary Cherry Doyle, in her pamphlet on Oconee county, Jocassee was the fair daughter of Chief Attakullakulla, powerful representative of his race in their treaties and dealings with pre-Revolutionary Carolinians. The writer also states that the Oconee (Brown Vipers) tribe lived on one side of the river and the Estato (Green Birds) on the other.

Between these rival tribes great enimity existed. But in spite of this animosity, Hagoochee, warrior of the Estato, often crossed the stream to hunt in Oconee territory. On one such adventure he fell and broke his leg. Lying there helpless and hopeless, he heard a clear voice singing. The singer was Jocassee, wandering alone in the woods. Touched by her enemy's plight, she secured help, had him carried to her home, and nursed him back to recovery.

Inevitably the young pair fell in love and became b e t r o t h e d. Chief Attakullakulla, perhaps out of devotion to his daughter, is said to have been kind to the Estato warrior; but his son was less amenable. Absent on a hunt while Nagoochee was recovering from his injury, the son returned to learn of his sister's betrothal and to vow he would have the life of Hagoochee. The latter, no doubt warned and aided by Jocassee, fled the brother's vengence but was overtaken and killed.

The chief's son swaggered home from his chase with the head of Jocassee's lover hanging from his belt. Never a word said, the stricken maiden, but stepped into a canoe and started silently down the river. When she reached midstream, she stepped from the boat and disappeared. Other maidens, watching, vowed that Jocassee did not sink under the water but walked on it to join Hagoochee, who beckoned to her from the opposite shore. That was the last seen of Jocassee, "the lost one."

Bartram's Travels in Oconee

The Keowee valley and the Oconee country have been made immortal by William Bartram, English botanist and explorer, who came to this country in 1773 and spent five years traveling and visiting the Indians. He recorded his impressions in delightful and gentle style in his "Travels" which was first published in 1791 and since then has been several times reprinted.

To read Bartram before visiting this hill country is to gain a perspective otherwise impossible. The beauties of the land and its vegetation take on new interest and color. In Bartram's day flourishing Indian villages dotted the countryside, and in them he was entertained with the guileless hospitality of a simple people.

He records also evidences of a far more ancient habitation than that of the Cherokee — mounds, ruins, and vestiges of cultivated fields. The explorer was told by the Indians that tales had been passed down by word of mouth, through all their generations, of how the first Indians in the region on their arrival from the West had found these silent witnesses of deserted settlements.

Today one searches in pain for the "incarnate fragrant strawberries" that so impressed Bartram and that he describes as spreading in "painted beds" over hundreds of acres in present Oconee county. But the section is still a rich field for botanists.

A Rediscovered Plant

In Jocassee, along in the 1880's was rediscovered the shortia, a long lost and even now almost unknown, alpine plant, resembling and closely akin to the galax. The glossy leaves of the shortia are more oval in form, and grow from the end of the stem, whereas the round galax leaf is attached to its stem in the center. The shortia has a shell pink blossom that shyly raises its head above its moist bed of leaf mold in late spring and early summer.

More than one story is told of its rediscovery; only that applying to Jocassee will be given here.

According to this version, a group of botanists, in the 1880's, were gathered at Highlands, collecting plants. One of the group said that he had seen in Paris, among the notes of Michaux, the French botanist who came to America shortly after the Repolutionary war, a description of a plant that he would like to find but had never seen. Michaux described the plant, the man continued, but recorded it merely as from the high mountains of North Carolina.

That very day one of the scouts brought in from Jocassee Valley a new specimen which was immediately acclaimed as that described by Michaux. It was named Shortia, in honor of Doctor Short, then a noted scientist and professor at Louisville Medical college.

Shortia is found in abundance in Jocassee Valley, growing beside springs and streamlets in shady places, and quantities of it are now being shipped elsewhere. Two Columbians, recent visitors in the Valley, brought home generous specimens of shortia to be planted in the botanical gardens of the University of South Carolina.

Jocassee As A Resort

To most low country folk, Jocassee Valley is known only as the site of Camp Jocassee, where this summer 50 girls at a time from eight states have been happy under the guidance of Miss Sarah Goldbolt. Miss Godbolt has conducted Camp Jocassee for 15 years, having been counsellor there for five consecutive years before that.

Those who have made their way from Pickens or Walhalla, past Salem and Tamassee, the D.A.R. school for girls, to lovely Jocassee, know that, besides the camp, there are comfortable accommodations for summer visitors at Attakulla Lodge, Riverview Lodge — both, like the camp set on luxurians lawns only a few feet from the river — and in numerous cottages. Some of the latter are to be had furnished at reasonable rent, the others occupied by the owners. Jocassee is still a little too difficult of access, due to rough roads, to have become spoiled by too many summer visitors, but the trip is worth the effort for the discriminating. No telephone startles the ear in this mountain vale, no radio profanes the quiet. Here the tired city dweller is soothed and reassured with eternal verities by the ceaseless music of the stream, as it dashes and ripples over its rocky bed undisturbed by wars and rumors of wars.

For those to whom the esthetic does not appeal, there are swimming in the natural pools of the crystal river water, mountain hikes, horseback rides, and the delights of Oconee state park within easy distance.

W. M. BROWN, formerly of
Charlotte, sage of Jocassee Valley

PLATE 287 *Oconee-bells - Shortia galacifolia* MVW

130

Jocassee Valley: Truth and Legend

The Keowee Courier – Walhalla, South Carolina – Tuesday, November 23, 1965
(original photographs reproduced; captions and article transcribed for readability)

These photos show scenes in Jocassee Valley soon to be covered with waters from the Duke Power project. Friendly Henry Haggerty (shown below) is full of history of the valley and as caretaker of Jocassee Camp for Girls is on hand every day for a friendly chat. In the first picture, the valley from a lookout is shown for its length. This property is owned by Ralph Alexander of Seneca. The second photograph is of the camp itself taken just across the lake from the main building and recreation hall. This property will be covered with approximately 285 feet of water.

Jocassee Valley Has Enough History To Fill Many Books Of Truth And Legend

It is hard to believe that here, where just a few short weeks ago laughter and antics of girl campers swayed the needles of the tall pines and echoed through the valley, is land that will be lost to many fathoms of water. In this very place, fish will sway the quiet waters 285 feet below the surface. Ground once swelling with laughter will be filled . . . furnishing power to gigantic plants and homes, bringing added wealth from a community that has one of the richest histories of anywhere in the United States.

The Keowee-Toxaway project proposed by Duke Power Company, will create two large lakes in the vicinity when massive dams are built to secure more generating plants for the company. Lake Toxaway will cover the area including Jocassee Valley. Lake Keowee, the second reservoir, will cover land near Seneca.

131

Jocassee Valley, as full of legend as the rest of Oconee County, lies seven miles above Salem nestled along the waters of the beautiful Whitewater River. Jocassee is a valley of fertile land, growing crops and livestock for its owners for generations, as well as affording the recreational activities so well-known.

This low bridge was built and is maintained by the county for the use of property owners in Jocassee Valley. Standing at one end it will be noticed the bridge is not built level to the water giving it a strength which would not be there is built as most bridges. Lower up stream affords heavy water, logs and debris to flow over the bridge forcing it down rather than up to be washed away.

Here in this picturesque valley, surrounded by mountains of the Blue Ridge range, lies a playground available for girls interested in camping and is often the recreation center for picnic-laden families from all over the two Carolinas.

Camp Jocassee has been the summer camp haven for hundreds of girls from all over the eastern United States, who have visited the camp year after year to enjoy its fine facilities.

Founded in 1922 by Miss Sarah Godbold of Columbia, the camp is owned by Mrs. Lucy Brown of Walhalla. The massive Brown building, built in 1946 by W. O. Brown, is the largest of the camp's building. It is built of lumber kiln-dried on the premises. Various other cabins bear names of near-by mountains — Bootleg, Cave, Double Springs. The recreation hall jutting out over water was heavily damaged in 1959. Containing a full-sized basketball court interior complete with stage at one end, the hall was smashed to the floor by the weight of ice and snow. But rebuilding was started early in the spring and the camp was again ready to receive its girls at the beginning of the 1960 summer season. Mr. Henry Haggerty is the bewhiskered 73-year-old gentleman who is custodian for the camp and resides there throughout the year. When Duke Power Company builds its planned dam, the camp, among other landmarks, will lie 285 feet under water.

W. O. Brown

W. O. Brown, father of Arthur Brown, first established a summer resort in the valley in 1898. He bought for himself and his family a 10-room home from Henry Glazener, a great uncle, and rented rooms to vacationers during the summer months.

Mr. Haggerty, a native of the region, is a springhtly 73 years of age and admits his hobby includes visiting with people passing through.

Attakulla Lodge houses more history than most museums. Built in the late 1800's, it has housed summer vacationers for most of its life. It stands three stories tall, but will also be lost to the waters of progress.

Carports are built differently today, but this old building served its purpose as a buggy shed and storehouse for many, many years. The age of the building is unknown, but is one of few left to be viewed by the public.

Within a short time, he found his home too crowded with people who were finding Jocassee Valley an ideal summer resort. So he added 20 rooms to the already three-story structure and created Attakulla Lodge. Mr. Brown ran a trading post in conjunction with the lodge and Brown children remember it as the gathering place of everyone in the valley. The Browns stayed in Jocassee until 1906, when they moved to Walhalla, leasing the lodge to hired help until 1914, when Silas Hinkle leased the entire layout and ran the resort spot for several years.

In August of 1916, Toxaway Dam in North Carolina burst and flood waters nearly destroyed Attakulla Lodge. Eighteen inches of mud lay on its floors with all fixtures and furniture ruined by mud and water, doing an estimated 7 or 8 thousand dollars worth of damage. But the clamor of Jocassee's vacationing friends decided the Brown family to once again put the inn into shape for the enjoyment of all those who came each summer.

In years since the lodge has ceased to function as an inn and has become a private hom. The C. O. Williams family now occupies it.

Jocassee History

The lodge takes its name from Attakulla, great chief of the Cherokees living on Whitewater River. With him lived his lovely daughter, Jocassee. Hence, the name of the valley. Legend has it that many years ago two tribes of Indians living in these mountains were engaged in a feud. Jocassee was in love with one of the Indians of the tribe which lived at that time on Eastotoe Creek, a few miles from his point, and one day while one of Jocassee's brothers was out on a hunt through the mountains, they came in contact with each other, and the young brother succeeded in scalping his sister's lover.

After doing so he put the scalp in his belt, returning to his tribe. As he was going up the Whitewater River he met his sister and father, who were wading. (The point is not known exactly.) The young man, it is said, was in a canoe, and after meeting his father and sister, they were taken into the canoe.

After going a short distance, in the middle of the stream, Jocassee jumped from the canoe and was drowned. The valley was named after this Indian maid, who buried herself in the crystal waters of Whitewater River when she recognized the scalp in her brother's belt as that of her lover.

As one wanders down the valley there is evidence that it was at one time the resort of those of means. The stately old "cottages" are of the size and victorian styling to suggest large familieis, gay parties — everything on a large scale.

The rambling picnic areas sprawl along the riverbank suggesting bountiful fare for a lazy summer day.

Brown Homeplace

Leaving the valley and returning to S.C. highway 11, the massive old Brown home is dominantly situated at the intersection, once echoing the sound of children's laughter and running feet during carefree summer days. For many years the summer home of the Arthur Brown family, it was abandoned in 1943 when a Brown son who was most interested in the home was killed in the war. Since then the huge house has been subjected to the weather and has reached a state of disrepair. However, it stands as a monument to the times. It, too, will succumb to the rising waters of Lake Toxaway.

The Brown home shown here was built near 100 years ago but has not been used by the family since 1943. It is a huge house and stands at the entrance of Jocassee Valley.

Chapman's Bridge

Continuing on S.C. highway 11 for two miles on a stretch of highway dedicated to William Holcombe, an early resident of the valley, one comes upon Chapman's Bridge, one of the two remaining covered bridges in the county. Spanning the Keowee River, of which Whitewater is a tributary, the 130 feet long structure was built in 1923, replacing the original bridge which was washed away when Toxaway Dam broke and flooded the valley. Built by local residents under James B. Craig, a contractor from Pickens, the bridge cost $6000, the cost split by Oconee and Pickens counties. Built primarily for horse-drawn carriages, the bridge is crossed daily by automobiles — many people out of curiosity. It is truly a picturesque sight — straight out of New England.

Being only 15 miles from its line, North Carolina tried to claim the bridge in 1963. However, Senator Marshall Parker placed this bridge and Prather's Brdige on the Tugaloo River under the care of the South Carolina Highway Department to insure upkeep.

The structures throughout the valley are reminders of by-gone days, standing to the memories of those who enjoyed the summer resort so often.

And some day soon it will be gone forever — covered with water which eventually will afford a new generation years of summer fun and activity. Admittedly, it will be different from that of our parents and grandparents.

Turning right at the Brown home and driving two miles will bring the travelers to Chapman's Bridge, one of three covered bridges left in South Carolina. Taken over by the state highway department in 1960, it will be preserved and is in an excellent state of repair.

134

Dam It!

In November, 1966, *The Greenville News* wrote a series of three articles concerning Duke Power's dam projects, seeking to explain what was – to us – unexplainable.

DUKE'S KEOWEE SPAN TO BE
TWICE AS LONG AS TWO SISTER DAMS

The Greenville News
November 17, 1966

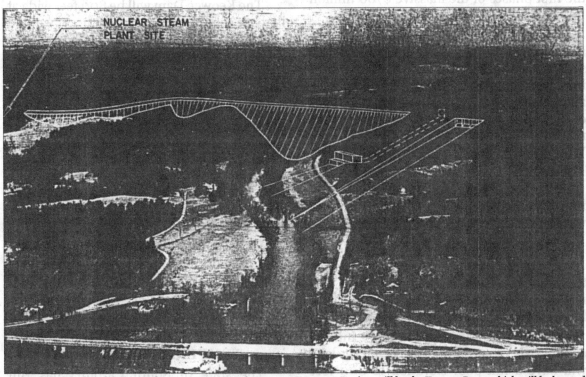

One of the key dams in Duke Power Company's Keowee-Toxaway Project will be the Keowee Dam, which will be located just a short distance northwest of where Highway 183 (in foreground) presently crosses the Keowee River southwest of Pickens. The dam, drawn into position by Duke engineers on the aerial photo of the dam site, will be 3,430 feet in length, 170 feet high, and will contain 1.9 million cubic yards of earth. The Oconee Nuclear Steam Generating Station is indicated by an arrow, and the hydro powerhouse will be behind the east corner of the dam. The dotted lines indicate the underground tunnel that will feed water from Lake Keowee into the turbines for generation purposes. The drawing to the right of the powerhouse is the spillway gates that will discharge excess water on occasions.

EDITOR'S NOTE: This is the first in a series of three articles that will reveal detailed facts and figures about the three dams that will help make up the Duke Power Co., Keowee-Toxaway Project in Pickens and Oconee counties. Each article will be accompanied by an aerial photograph on which Duke Power's design engineers have drawn in exact location of the dams, powerhouses and pumped storage facilities.

How much is 669 billion gallons of water?

It's enough to supply the daily requirements, at present consumption rates, of the cities of Spartanburg, Greenville and Anderson – for 40 years.

It's also the amount of water that will be impounded in the two lakes that will help form Duke Power Company's Keowee-Toxaway Project in Pickens and Oconee counties.

This is one of the interesting facts that are beginning to sift out of engineering slide rules as Duke Power readies itself to begin building the first phases of the massive $700 million Keowee-Toxaway Project early next year.

The project will combine hydro-electric and pumped storage generation with nuclear steam generation, with the two impoundments to be known as Lake Jocassee and Lake Keowee. Lake Jocassee, the upper of the two reservoirs, will be formed by four rivers that headwater in North Carolina – the Whitewater, Thompson, Horsepasture and Toxaway.

Waters released from Jocassee will drain into Lake Keowee, which will receive other water from Cane Creek and the Little River.

TWICE AS LONG

The Keowee Dam will be twice as long as the other two dams in the project at 3,500 feet, 20 feet higher than the Little River Dam, but 215 lower than the lofty Jocassee Dam.

The Keowee Dam will contain 2 million cubic yards of earth, and the resulting lake will have a full pool elevation of 800 feet above sea level. The license agreement with the Federal Power Commission will allow the lake to be drawn down a maximum of 25 feet.

The surface area of Lake Keowee, when full will be 18,100 acres, and this will provide 300 miles of shoreline – more than South Carolina has in beach area bordering the Atlantic Ocean.

The Keowee Dam will contain two 70,000 kilowatt conventional hydro-electric units for a total of 140,000 kilowatts of generating capacity.

The waterwheel turbines which will turn the generators will be fed water through a tunnel 800 feet long and 33.5 feet in diameter. This tunnel alone, when full, will contain 5.3 million gallons of water.

800 feet wide

The Keowee Dam will be 800 feet wide at its base, about the same length as two and two-thirds football fields laid end to end, and 20 feet wide at the top.

Duke Power is presently committed to maintain a minimum continuous downstream flow of 152 cubic feet of water per second, but the average flow will be 1,000 cubic feet per second. The 152 cubic feet is the lowest stream flow ever recorded on the Keowee River, and Duke engineers say that more than that amount will be released without any effort due to normal discharge through the gates.

Duke and the Army Corps of Engineers are now working out a flow agreement that will be compatible with possible projects at Middleton Shoals, Trotters Shoals, and the completed federal projects at Hartwell and Clark Hill on the Savannah River.

TEMPERATURE CHECKS

The state of South Carolina has run temperature checks on the Keowee River at a point just below where the Jocassee Dam will be built, and the lowest water temperature ever recorded was 37 degrees (January) and the highest 78 (August).

WATER OF RIVER TO FLOW BACKWARD

The Greenville News
November 23, 1966

The Jocassee Dam, which will impound the Lake Jocassee portion of Duke Power Company's Keowee-Toxaway project, will be the highest dam in South Carolina. The dam will be 385 feet in height, 1,750 feet in length, and will require about 7,200,000 cubic yards of rockfill to build. Lake Jocassee will impound 7,400 surface acres of water within 75 miles of shoreline. State Highway 11, at right in the photo, will be inundated on the south side of Jocassee Dam by Lake Keowee. The sketch in the photo shows the Jocassee Powerhouse, and the dotted lines indicate the tunnels through which water will be fed into the turbines for hydroelectric generation. Water will be pumped back through these same tunnels at night for reuse the next day. The covered bridge over the Keowee River in center-foreground, called the Chapman Bridge, is one of few covered bridges remaining in service in South Carolina. It will be removed before Lake Keowee fills.

EDITOR'S NOTE: This is the second in a series of three articles that will reveal detailed facts and figures about the three dams and two lakes that will help make up Duke Power Company's Keowee-Toxaway Project in Pickens and Oconee counties. Each article will be accompanied by an aerial photograph on which Duke Power's Design Engineers have drawn in exact locations of the dams, powerhouses and pumped storage facilities.

The waters of mountain rivers seldom flow backwards, but with help from Duke Power Co. that's exactly what's going to happen when the generation facilities begin operating at Duke's Jocassee Dam on the Keowee River.

It will be through a type of hydroelectric generation known as pumped storage, and it's a relatively simple operation.

Reduced to its basics, here's how the Jocassee pumped storage installations will work:

Water falls through the turbines, turning the generators, and emerges into Lake Keowee. Later, when the demand for electricity on the Duke system is lighter, the turbogenerators are reversed, pumping water back into Lake Jocassee for reuse the following day.

This hydro-produced electricity is used to supply peaking power for the heavier system demands of the noon and early evening hours.

The water is pumped back into Lake Jocassee late at night or in the early morning hours, or on the weekend when demands on the Duke system are at their lightest. Electricity from Duke's steam-driven generating plants is used to drive the generators when they act as motors and turn the turbines into pumps.

PUMPING ACTION

This pumping action isn't likely to cause any extreme fluctuation of Lake Jocassee's surface level. This fluctuation, due to pumping, is likely to be between two and four feet in any one week, under normal conditions, with six feet the extreme figure.

There eventually will be three of these reversible pump-turbines at the Jocassee Dam, each rated at 150,000 kilowatts, plus a single conventional hydro unit rated at 160,000 kilowatts.

The pumped storage installation at Jocassee will be Duke Power's first. Duke engineers say that the tributaries of the Keowee River, such as the Toxaway, Horsepasture, and Whitewater Rivers, also contain sites that may be suitable for other pumped storage installations if future demands and economic conditions warrant their construction.

The two tunnels carrying water to Jocassee's four turbines will be 900 feet in length and 32.5 feet in diameter, and maximum drawdown of the lake's surface will be 30 feet.

Jocassee Dam will be the highest ever built in South Carolina, and one of the highest in the southeast. It will be 385 feet in height, 1,750 feet in length, and will require 7,200,000 cubic yards of rockfill in construction.

The dam will be 1,200 feet wide at its base, or the length of four football fields laid end to end, and will be 20 feet wide at its top.

75-MILE SHORELINE

The resulting Lake Jocassee will have 75 miles of shoreline, and will be surrounded by more than 60,000 acres of mountain land that will be under game management by the S.C. Wildlife Resources Department. Hunting for deer, bear and turkey will be allowed when suitable populations of these species have been built up – not for at least five years.

Although covering only a little more than one-third the surface area of Lake Keowee, Lake Jocassee will contain considerably more water impounded between the mountains which form its shores. Jocassee will contain 373 billion gallons of water at full pond, while Keowee, broader and shallower, will contain 296 billion gallons when full.

Most of the Lake Jocassee shoreline will be inaccessible by road, and the steepness of the terrain coupled with the difficulties of building all-weather roads may severely limit the possibilities of recreational lease lots. Most of these lots, which Duke Power will make available to the public on a first come-first served basis after the lakes fill, will be around more accessible Lake Keowee.

At last count Duke Power had made 5,212 recreational lot leases to individuals on its various lakes.

Whereas the Lake Keowee basin, covering 18,000 acres, will be completely cleared of trees, the Lake Jocassee basin will be cleared of trees only from the 990 (feet above sea level) mark to the full pond mark of 1,110 feet.

Sixty percent of the marketable timber has been removed from the Keowee basin and 40 per cent from the Jocassee basin. Lumbering operations, using local contractors, are now harvesting 15 million board feet of timber and about 15,000 cords of pulpwood annually.

(Next: Little River Dam and the connecting canal).

LINKING CANAL REPRESENTS
MAJOR CHORE AT DAM SITE

The Greenville News
December 1, 1966

The Little River dam will join with the Keowee Dam in forming Lake Keowee, the 18,100 acre lower impoundment of Duke Power's Keowee-Toxaway electric generating complex. There will be no hydro generation at the Little River Dam, northwest of Newry (in foreground). The dam will serve to impound the lower portion of Lake Keowee, with that portion being connected to the Keowee River portion by a canal just west of the Keowee Dam. The Little River Dam, shown in position by this Duke Power drawing on an aerial photo of the area, will be 150 feet high, 2140 feet in length, and will contain 1.4 million cubic yards of earth.

EDITOR'S NOTE: This is the last in a series of three articles that have revealed detailed facts and figures about the three dams and two lakes that will help make up Duke Power Company's Keowee-Toxaway project in Pickens and Oconee counties. Each article has been accompanied by an aerial photograph on which Duke Power's design engineers drew in exact location of the dams, powerhouses and pumped storage facilities.

It won't be in the same class as the Panama or Suez, of course, but the canal that Duke Power Co. will dig to connect the two basins that will form its Lake Keowee in Pickens and Oconee counties still will be a considerable chore.

The Little River and Cane Creek will feed water into the lower, southwest segment of Lake Keowee, while the Keowee River and its tributaries will fill the upper basin. A canal connecting the two basins will be dug just west of the Keowee Dam on the Keowee River.

A second dam, to be called the Little River Dam, will be constructed just north of the town of Newry. This dam will have no power generation function, and its purpose is merely to impound the lower basin of Lake Keowee.

While the connecting canal is in a naturally low saddle of land running between the two basins, Duke engineers still expect to have to remove about 665,000 cubic yards of earth to get the necessary depth for proper water flow between the basins. This dirt will be used in the Keowee Dam.

This is the second largest earth removal job in the entire Keowee-Toxaway project. The excavation for the Jocassee powerhouse yard, the water intake, spillway and tailrace installations, will require the excavation and removal of more than 2,500,000 cubic yards of earth.

The Keowee powerhouse yard will require excavation of 500,000 cubic yards. The Oconee Nuclear Generating Station's powerhouse yard will necessitate the excavation of 466,000 cubic yards of dirt, and the station's discharge canal will require the removal of an additional 480,000 cubic yards of dirt.

This totals close to 5,000,000 cubic yards of earth that must be excavated for initial phases of Duke's Keowee-Toxaway project.

The Little River Dam is the smallest and lowest of the three dams in the project. It will be 150 feet in height, 1,750 feet in length, and will contain 1,600,000 cubic yards of earthfill. Base width will be 800 feet, and at the top it will be the widest of the three dams at 32 feet.

Reason for the extra width of the Little River Dam is that it will serve as the base for a heavy duty road that will be used to transport construction materials to the Oconee Nuclear Generating Station.

LOCAL ECONOMY IMPACT

Duke expects local expenditures during construction to be sizeable. The Keowee Dam and its hydro installation will require a peak work force of 500 men with an average payroll of 300 men for the three-year construction period beginning next year.

This work force will add about $10 million to the area's economy during construction, $6 million in salaries and $4 million in materials and services.

The Oconee Nuclear Station will require a peak construction force of nearly 1,000 men, and Jocassee hydro development is expected to demand a peak force of 600 men. The nuclear plant will account for $30 million in construction payroll, Jocassee $7 million — for a grand total of $43 million in construction salaries to be paid.

In addition, wives and other members of construction force families will be available to the local labor markets. Many of these will be able to fill specialized positions, such as teaching, secretarial or clerical.

The first two hydroelectric developments and the initial nuclear generating station will require a staff of about 170 persons as permanent operating and maintenance force with an estimated annual payroll of about $1.2 million.

In addition to personnel associated with electric generating plants, other Duke employees would be engaged in work relating to recreation, water quality, insect control, timber and pulpwood operations and land management. The payroll for this type work plus additional supplies and services secured locally and associated with these activities is expected to add another $200,000 annually to the local economy.

Business that will be generated locally by the Duke Power project will be considerable. In addition to the 210 persons to be permanently employed by Duke, forestry operations are expected to generate 200 jobs for woods workers employed by private sawmill and timber operators.

At least 40 additional jobs will be provided by lessees and operators of marinas and other recreational facilities. Thus, the initial phases of the project will create about 450 new jobs in project-related activities.

Applying the ratios developed by the United States Chamber of Commerce it can be determined that these 450 jobs will infuse $3 million in new personal income into the local economy, $1.5 million in new bank deposits, 345 additional jobs in other fields, $1.8 million in new retail sales per year, mortgages or rent on 525 homes or apartments, and ownership of 540 passenger cars.

2,000 WORKERS

Construction employment on the fully developed $700 million project will fluctuate, but including Duke and non-Duke payrolls directly engaged in project activities, an estimated 2,000 persons will ultimately be involved.

Supplementing the contributions of other reservoirs in the Savannah River Basin, Lake Keowee and Jocassee will offer superb opportunities for development of attractive tourist facilities. Lake Keowee will be only 26 miles from Greenville and 24 miles from Anderson – within easy commuting distance for summer fun seekers.

The four-county area nearest Lake Keowee and Jocassee (Anderson, Greenville, Oconee and Pickens) has a current population of about 425,000. This is expected to reach 610,000 by 1980, and this burgeoning population will make extensive use of Keowee and Jocassee for recreational purposes.

These developments also should attract a number of visitors from further afield, just as Lake Norman, Duke's newest power impoundment near Charlotte, NC, is now being visited by many midwesterners. Lake Jocassee, nestled high in the southern Appalachian mountains in an extremely scenic setting, should prove highly attractive to out-of-state tourists as well as Carolinians.

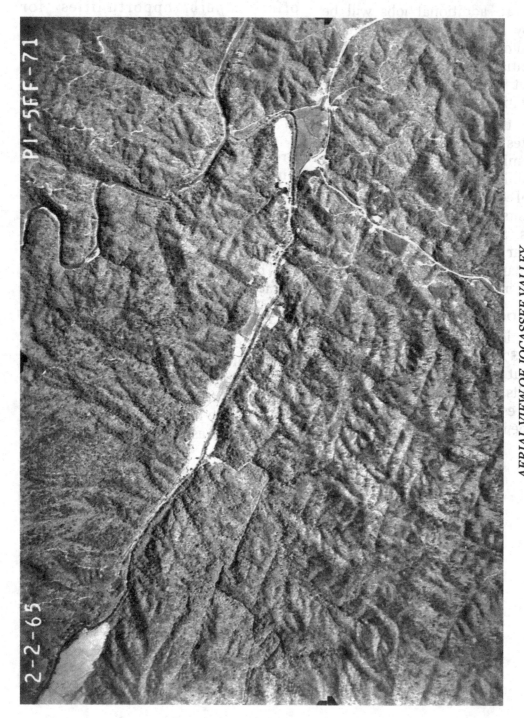

AERIAL VIEW OF JOCASSEE VALLEY
2-2-65
(Following page is same view on present map of Lake Jocassee)

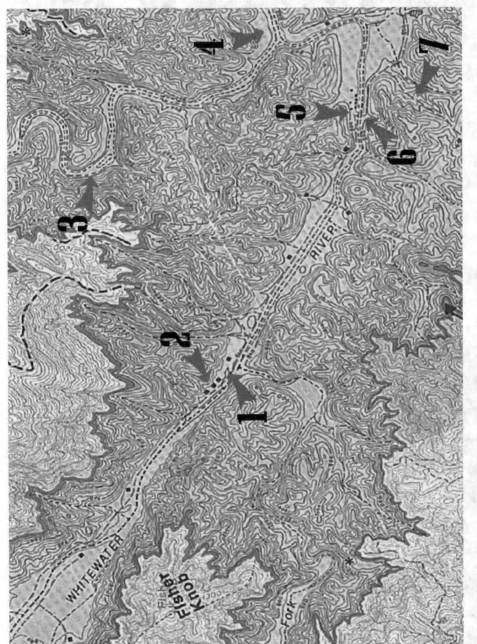

1. *Jocassee International Airport,* at the intersection of Whitewater River and Devil's Fork Creek
2. *Bowling Alley* (left); *Attakulla Lodge* (center); *spring house* (right); *barn* (far right)
3. *Toxaway River* snakes around the mountain
4. Toxaway and Whitewater Rivers form *Keowee River*
5. *Camp Jocassee for Girls*
6. *Steel Bridge crosses Whitewater River* (Off the Wall Diving has established a technical dive site to the bridge and portions of the Girls Camp)
7. *Old roadbed* which leads up the mountain to Devil's Fork State Park

(Map courtesy of Atlantic Mapping, Inc.)

143

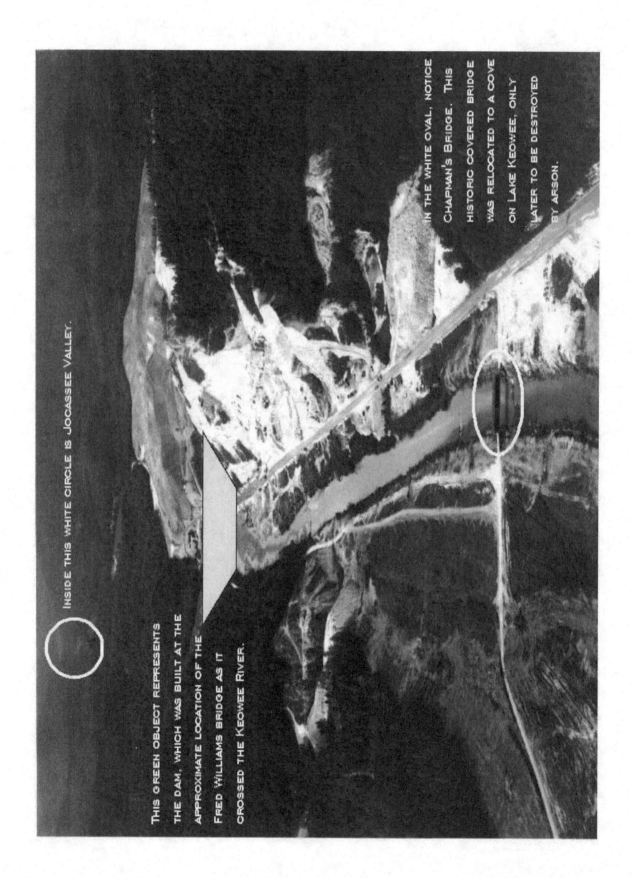

INSIDE THIS WHITE CIRCLE IS JOCASSEE VALLEY.

THIS GREEN OBJECT REPRESENTS THE DAM, WHICH WAS BUILT AT THE APPROXIMATE LOCATION OF THE FRED WILLIAMS BRIDGE AS IT CROSSED THE KEOWEE RIVER.

IN THE WHITE OVAL, NOTICE CHAPMAN'S BRIDGE. THIS HISTORIC COVERED BRIDGE WAS RELOCATED TO A COVE ON LAKE KEOWEE, ONLY LATER TO BE DESTROYED BY ARSON.

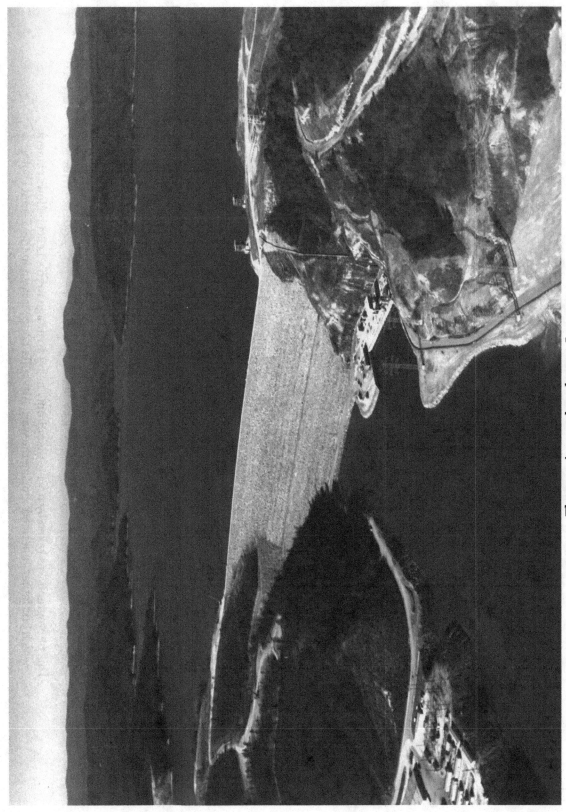

The massive earthen dam at Jocassee

Here Lies Jocassee Valley

This photograph was taken by my brother Jimmy using a vintage 1930's Leika bellows camera which our father "liberated" during the war. Attakulla Lodge is seen in the distant center.

Whippoorwill Farewell

Jocassee Valley was magnificent from the air. What freedom in being able to soar like an eagle over the serene Valley and catch glimpses of Upper and Lower Whitewater Falls from a perspective few were privileged to see!

The Whippoorwill saw it.

Every night at supper, somewhere between the fried chicken and cornbread, between the sweet tea and blackberry cobbler, someone would "sshhh" everyone, and we would listen to the Whippoorwill heralding his nightly sojourn up and down the Valley. I've often thought about the Whippoorwill in the years since the flooding. Did he find his way up to a higher mountain top as the water rose to inundate his peaceful domain? Somehow, I believe — I need to believe — that he still listens for our "sshhh" at suppertime, but now hears only his own familiar call echoing across the deep waters of Lake Jocassee. While most dreamers imagine a ghost Princess gently paddling across the lake, I listen intently for the call of the Whippoorwill.

~

During our 1998 camping trip on the shores of Lake Jocassee, my husband Dave and I were just falling asleep when I heard the Whippoorwill's song — and my heart stirred. I poked Dave and said, "Listen! Do you hear that? It's the Whippoorwill!" I closed my eyes and imagined we were eating supper at the Lodge. It was a wonderful experience! The next morning, I remarked again about hearing the Whippoorwill. Dave said, "I thought that bird would *never* hush!" Indeed, the bird did not cease calling until the *wee* hours of the morning. I guess he had a lot to tell me.

On that same camping trip, I came to the painful realization that Jocassee Valley is lost forever. I have tried to accept the lake for its obvious beauty, but I don't believe I'll return there for a while. It reminds me of what has been sacrificed in the name of "progress." I've watched boats swiftly slicing through the water 300 feet above Attakulla Lodge's resting place, knowing that the passengers were not aware of — and perhaps did not care about — the paradise buried deep below. And it *is* still there. Unlike most other structures in the Valley, the Lodge was not demolished before the flooding began. Buck and Fred flew over the lake as it was filling and thought they saw the Lodge upside down, caught in the trees near Devil's Fork. It broke their hearts. When I visited the lake, I wondered if the obviously man-made debris I saw on the shore is a piece of the Lodge which has managed to float to the surface. I felt sad.

Recent events, however, may prove that the Lodge is standing. Bill Routh of *Off the Wall Dive Charters* and I were studying pictures of Attakulla Lodge and noted the interior chimney which might be anchoring her to the lake bottom. A surveyor's plat of my family's property will soon be converted to GPS coordinates, and an expedition with an underwater camera may finally reveal her fate. I feel hopeful.

Dot Jackson once told me that "a place is yours until someone takes it and does what they want to with it ... then it isn't yours anymore." Jimmy and I have pondered what Jocassee would be like today, if it had not been flooded. We know, realistically, it would not be the valley we knew. The end of the Valley would be a golf course, with condos dotting the entire mountainside ... and, of course, there would be a bus transporting inner-tubers from here to there. The Jocassee Valley we knew, had it not been drowned, would have been seriously compromised, "like watching a slow death," Jimmy said. "Maybe a quick death," he speculates, "was better." Our memories may be God's way of sparing us that pain.

Perhaps Ron Rash, in his poem "Deep Water" expresses it best:

> *Soon that squared pool of water flickers as if a mirror,*
> *surfaces memory of when this deep water was a sky.*

The Cherokee nation must have mourned their loss as we have. *The Keowee Trail* recounts their plight:

> *Knew they then that all was ended,*
> *Gone were lands that they deemed sacred;*
> *Gone the lands that they had fought for,*
> *Gone the lands their fathers died for,*
> *Gone the lands they gave their lives for;*
> *Gone to them forevermore.*

148

Chief Attakullakulla, writing to John Stuart, a British agent, said:

> *I will eat and drink with my white brothers, and will expect friendship and good usage from them. It is but a little spot that you ask, and I am willing that your people should live upon it. I pity the white people, but they do not pity me . . . The Great Being above is very good, and provides for everybody . . . he gave us this land, but the white people seem to want to drive us from it.*

Jane Yolen, in her book <u>Letting Swift River Go</u>, speaks of a town going through the agony of being transformed as was Jocassee:

> *The drowning of the Swift River towns*
> *to create the Quabbin was not a unique event.*
> *The same story – only with different names –*
> *has occurred all over the world*
> *wherever nearby large cities have had powerful thirsts.*
> *Such reservoirs are trade-offs, which, like all trades,*
> *are never easy, never perfectly fair.*

In the end, the story's character writes:

> *When it got dark, the stars came out, reflecting in the water, winking on and off and on like fireflies. I leaned over the side of the boat and caught the starry water in my cupped hands. For a moment I remembered the wind through the willow, the trains whistling on Rabbit Run, the crossroads where I had met Georgie Warren and Nancy Vaughan. Gone, all gone, under the waters.*
>
> > *Then I heard my mother's voice coming to me over the drowned years. "You have to let them go, Sally Jane." I looked down into the darkening deep,*
> >
> > *smiled,*
> >
> > *and did.*

So, I'll long remember the Whippoorwill's familiar call that night as a wonderful, comforting memory, but *for now . . .*

Whippoorwill, farewell.

Our first glimpse of Attakulla Lodge – 300 feet underwater --showing the rafters of the sloped roof on the kitchen at the back of the house (see page 44). On the right, notice the line which the diver is permanently securing to the corner post.

We Have Structure!

Everyone needs heroes. Here's the story of mine.

I got a phone call one evening from a friend who said, "I have Bill Routh on the phone. He owns a diving company and would like to talk to you about the Lodge." Bill introduced himself by saying he had heard there was a hotel in Jocassee Valley before it was flooded.

"Yes, that was my family's home – Attakulla Lodge," I replied.

"Well, I'm interested in looking for it," said Bill.

"It's not there anymore."

"Why do you say that?" he inquired.

"My uncles flew over the lake as it was filling and saw the Lodge turned upside down, hung up in the trees over by Devil's Fork."

Bill asked, "What makes them think it was the Lodge?"

Not having a direct answer, I replied, "I don't know . . . I'll call and ask."

The next day I phoned Uncle Fred and asked what they saw. Apparently, the lake was about 60 feet deep as they flew over. The Lodge stood 30 feet at the apex of the roof. Peering down through the water, they couldn't see the Lodge's shadowy image. Besides, "we saw floor over by Devil's Fork – just floor." They assumed that she had lifted off her foundation and floated a while before entangling in the trees, upside down.

I telephoned Bill and relayed the news. He said he'd still like to meet and look at some pictures; so, one Sunday night on his way through Columbia, we met, spreading photos of Jocassee all over the restaurant table. Bill's eyes widened at the wealth of information I had accumulated. "Man, I wish I'd had some of this stuff when we were searching for Camp Jocassee!" Bill exclaimed.

While he ate, I shared about the Lodge – what it was like to visit her as a child – and how terribly I missed being able to go there. Perusing through the documents and photos, a couple of things soon caught his eye.

151

"Did the Lodge have a fireplace?"

"Yes, it had fireplaces on both floors," I replied, wondering what difference that could make. He explained that a masonry chimney, which goes all the way from the ground through the roof, could very well be anchoring the Lodge to the bottom. That, plus the fact that the lake filled slowly, allowing her timbers to soak up water and become heavier, was in our favor. With Bill's knowledge of how underwater structures behave, he felt there was an excellent chance she was right where we left her. As we were wrapping up, another item caught his careful eye.

"D-e-b-b-i-e," he said slowly, hoping that he was really seeing what he *thought* he was seeing. "What is that?"

"That's a survey of my family's property. I got it from Duke when I went up there."

"That shows the coordinates of your land. We can have these converted to GPS coordinates and go right to where the Lodge is in the lake!"

I could see the excitement in his eyes, and for the first time, I had some hope that I might actually see Attakulla Lodge again. Many things affect the visibility in the lake, the time of year being one of them. It would soon be getting too cold to dive that deep, so we'd have to wait until summer 2004. The waiting was the hard part.

~

The time finally arrived to actively plan our hunting expedition. Bill got in touch with Stephen R. Edwards, a Salem surveyor who uses his interest in the history of an area to survey and research property boundaries. Bill gave him the known coordinates of several locations in the lake – among them the *Mt. Carmel Cemetery* and *Camp Jocassee for Girls* – which assisted Stephen in meticulously converting the coordinates on my family's plat to GPS coordinates. His obvious love for what he does and his interest in our project was proven by his sole request for compensation: a copy of my book, which Bill gratefully provided.

Now I was beginning to feel pregnant with anticipation. Even though I continued to hear rumors that the Lodge had been seen floating in the lake, Bill steadily encouraged me that he hoped to find things as we expected. "Keep a positive attitude," he encouraged. "You wear it well." As the projected time drew near to take the boat to the site and drop a remote underwater camera, I became increasingly antsy. Any minute, Bill could call with the words "it's calm on the lake; get up here!" Surely the phone would ring any day now. And it did. On August 4, 2004.

I was just about to walk out of the house to go to work when the phone rang.

Bill asked, "Have you read your e-mail this morning?"

"Not yet. Did you send me something?"

"Go check your e-mail. I want you to read something while I'm on the phone."

Here are his words:

----- Original Message-----
From: Bill Routh
Sent: Wednesday, August 04, 2004 4:32 AM
To: Debbie Fletcher; Anna Simon; Charles Johnson; Jackie Smith; Steve Parker; Jason Parker; Bill Willard
Subject: Attakulla Lodge

Good Morning,

You might wonder why someone would sit down at 3:51 a.m. and write a letter. Well, the dog and the cat just can't give me the conversation and the excitement I long for at this hour. It has been almost two years since the discovery of the bridge and the pillars of Camp Jocassee. I have met several wonderful people since that time, but the one person who has stood out was Debbie Fletcher, granddaughter of the owner of the Attakulla Lodge. She met with me to show me pictures and offer information about the Girls Camp. During the meeting we talked about her book in the works, Jocassee Remembered. The information she had compiled was extensive. Within her boxes of research were two maps and a plat she had recovered from Duke Power Co. in Charlotte. I was amazed to see the information she had compiled. I began to look at the possibility of looking for the lodge and trying to put together a search plan to locate the site of the building. I was told by several eye witnesses and had heard of several accounts of the building floating around the lake during the early days the lake was filling up. The one thing I have learned is to be polite and listen to the information each person had to offer. I have not lost hope of the possibility the lodge had survived the flooding of the valley and stood proud today preserved by the depths of the lake and waiting for visitors to return as they had so many times before.

I have been patiently waiting for the weather to allow me to park the boat over the site and not be blown away in a few minutes. Today, at 2:08 a.m., August 4th 2004 I was able to look back in time and view the lodge as it stands today. This was accomplished with a remote camera and several hours of maneuvering the boat to try and pinpoint the location. I am as positive as I can be from 300 feet above that I have filmed the building. If I am wrong then I have located the bowling alley adjacent to the lodge. I wish the time of day was fitting to make several calls and announce this find. We are planning a dive this weekend to confirm the site and put to rest the rumors and offer first-hand information and with luck, video and pictures. Please understand that the efforts of several persons have made this possible, and I know the search would still be at the drawing table if it weren't for everyone involved. Please don't wait for a better time to call and talk about it. I can't wait for my phone to ring.

This effort was driven by the kind-hearted person that I have met in Debbie Fletcher. Her love and memories for the Attakulla Lodge has moved me to answer the questions of time. I hope the answer is as good as I have believed it to be. Bill

"Don't you want to come up here today and see the video?" Bill questioned, and I could hear the smile in his voice. My grown-up responsibilities got the best of me, and I *very* sadly declined.
"If you were 18, you'd get up here today!" he laughed.
"If I were 18, I wouldn't have a job!" I said, pleading my case.

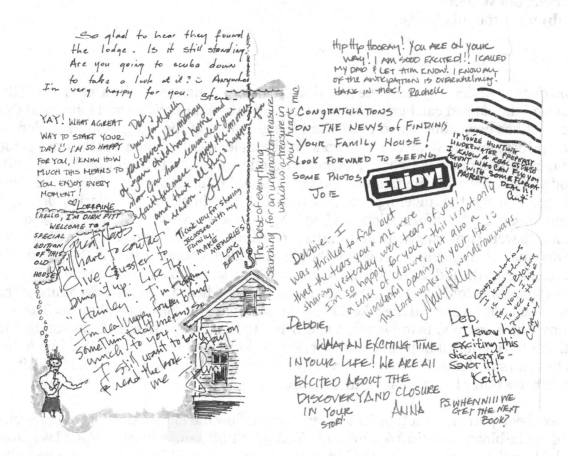

I couldn't wait to share this unbelievable news with my friends at work. Knowing how important finding Attakulla Lodge was to me, they threw me a surprise party that afternoon. Among the treasured mementos was a card they all signed. We laughed at the prospect of showcasing the Lodge on a special edition of "This Old House" – and cried as Mary Lou read this touching poem Betty wrote about the Lodge:

The Find

Hidden treasures to be found
Far beneath the water's edge.
Long, lost memories of days gone by
Nestled deep, but still very much within reach.

The sun comes up as do the emotions.
The divers, the media, the family;
Their hearts packed in there, too,
As they board the boat with underwater camera.
Ready to capture footage that will forever ring true.

At last, the Attakulla Lodge welcomes us to the river's floor,
300 feet below, it stands proud with open arms.

Today, you come back to life as we all knew you would.
Never forgotten with all your charm,
Under Lake Jocassee,
She protects you from all harm.

Good morning, Attakulla Lodge,
We see you standing there.
Thank you for the memories we hold in our hearts so dear.

Like the crystal clear waters that tuck you in each night,
Sweet dreams, Attakulla,
Whippoorwills will sing to you tonight.

- Betty Allen

The following Saturday, Dave and I met Bill at his shop. Jackie Smith and Charles Johnson had already arrived and were loading their gear onto the boat. Bill introduced us, and they expressed their excitement over this dive. They talked tech-talk with Bill about the dive, and I was so grateful they knew what they were doing. They liken themselves to equal parts astronaut, time traveler, and archaeologist. Jackie said, "We are always going looking for something (ships, buildings, cave systems) that disappeared a long time ago. We want to know what happened, how did they live, how did they die, what was their life like?"

According to Bill, Jackie, and Charles, technical mix diving is dangerous, requiring intense training which not many divers are willing to do. Jackie and Charles use *closed circuit rebreathers* (CCR), allowing them to adjust the mixture, or ratio, of oxygen, nitrogen, and helium, depending upon their depth. A CCR does not expel anything into the environment and is considered the ultimate gas management tool in diving. However, one tiny miscalculation, and you're dead. And why *helium*, you may ask? Well, think about chugging a martini on an empty stomach. OK . . . now think about chugging 5 martinis on an empty stomach! For the first 99 feet of dive depth, the diver experiences what feels like the effects of chugging one martini. For every additional 33 feet of depth, add the effects of another martini. You can imagine a diver's state of mind at 300 feet: totally intoxicated after chugging 7 martinis! The helium counteracts this narcotic effect and gives him a clear head.

Charles Johnson, Jackie Smith and Bill Routh study a
picture of Attakulla Lodge

"Wanna see a video?" Bill smiled with his whole face, not easily containing his excitement over the first video of the Lodge. Watching this underwater video was much like watching a parade through a knothole in a fence. Dangling a small camera from 300 feet of cable, on a drifting boat, in the middle of the night, alone, is no small task, either. At times, the camera angled in such a way that we were not sure what we were looking at, except that it was definitely a man-made structure. Wooden structures in the valley were demolished before flooding – except ours – so this had to be Attakulla Lodge. We could clearly see what looked like rafters, maybe the edge of the porch, definitely wood siding. The sight of a ghostly-looking tree, leafless and shrouded in white silt, was a silent reminder of the valley's demise. As Bill had said before, "Everything that was in the lake as it filled is still there, frozen in a time capsule." The white, powdery silt that blankets the lake bottom indeed looks like snow.

Bill shows me the GPS locator.

Bill briefs Charles and Jackie.

Bill's main concern was that the temporary line he had anchored to the Lodge had gotten snagged that night as he was pulling the camera back up. Although he had hit the *man overboard* GPS coordinates when he first sited the Lodge, we would still need to drop the line right onto the Lodge in order to make the dive as safe as possible for Jackie and Charles. At a depth of 300 feet, the water is approximately 40°, and it is pitch dark. With only the aid of flashlights, lines of rope are tied at various points for the divers to follow, much like breaking twigs to mark a trail. Losing your bearings at the bottom could mean death. Becoming disoriented, a diver might even lose the ability to determine which direction is up.

It was finally time to head out to the dive site which Bill had marked that night with a piece of driftwood. A buoy might have raised curiosity, causing someone to remove it. All eyes searched the top of the water until someone shouted, "There it is!" We boated over and attached a more obvious plastic buoy. *"Whew! That's one thing off my mind,"* I thought to myself. Admittedly, I was a bundle of emotions: excitement, nervousness, doubt, anticipation . . . my thoughts were like the surface of the lake – calm one minute, then disturbed the next. Part of me was afraid to admit that

The camera is carefully lowered.

We were glued to the TV monitor.

I just might experience one of the biggest let-downs of my life. The hustle of activity on the boat soon gave me something else to think about. The underwater camera, which is simply an inexpensive jury-rigged security camera attached to a very expensive cable attached to an even more expensive 500-watt bulb, had to be carefully lowered into the water, while we tracked its position on a TV monitor. Most of the trees at deeper depths were left in the lake, so avoiding getting snagged in one of them was of utmost concern.

I paced and fidgeted until finally Bill yelled, *"WE HAVE STRUCTURE!!"* The camera displayed the image we were desperately seeking: wood siding and an apparent hole in the roof. We were peering into a part of Attakulla Lodge which hadn't been seen in 33 years. GPS coordinates were recorded, additional cable was released to afford the slack needed to account for the boat drifting slightly, and the divers jumped into action. I marveled at the amount of equipment these guys need to wear to make a deep dive. They truly do look more like astronauts than divers.

Well-trained technical mix divers dive in teams, supported by a team of safety divers. While the mix divers go to the deep dive site, the safety divers (Bill Routh and Chris Salter on this dive) dive to an approximate depth of 30-60 feet and 150 feet, respectively. A 300-foot dive necessitates a one and one-half hour decompression stage, with the mix diver stopping at various intervals for extended periods of time. The safety divers note the exact time the mix divers hit the water and time their dive in order to meet the mix divers at the appropriate depth and time during the decompression trip back to the surface. Their role, according to Bill, is to provide assistance to the technical mix diver who might need help removing and transporting unneeded gear, thereby making the decompression "hang" more comfortable. Safety divers also supply backup equipment or oxygen in the event of a failure or emergency. If a problem occurs the safety diver can quickly surface to notify a helicopter for transport to a recompression chamber. "A good safety diver provides a *backup brain* for the diver who might make a mistake, and *eyes* to see problems the diver might not be aware of," explained Bill.

Chris Salter

Bill Routh

The boat was crowded with my family, the news crew, five divers, and a myriad of diving equipment. As Jackie and Charles readied themselves, I felt woefully inadequate. I wanted to help them do *something*, but I realized that these men were here to do something incredible for *me*. How many times had I grieved over the fact that I didn't fully appreciate my last visit to the Lodge. Yes, I was heartbroken knowing that I'd never return. But why didn't I think to just pick up some part of her to keep as a remembrance? If I could only see her one more time. These men were going to be my eyes. They would be the ones to confirm if Attakulla Lodge was still standing, or if we had found a debris field. As they prepared to enter the water, all I could think of to say was, "Be safe!"

The five minutes it took them to drop to the bottom seemed like an eternity. I finally sat down and intently watched the TV monitor to wait for a glimpse of something familiar. We could catch only bits and pieces from time to time, and I still didn't know if the Lodge was intact. The primary goal of this first dive was to visually confirm the building's condition and, hopefully, tie a permanent down line to the structure or to something sturdy nearby. Suddenly, I saw Charles's image appear on the monitor. He had something dangling from the crook of his elbow. We strained to see through

My daughter Pam and I study the monitor.

the glare on the screen when I exclaimed, "What is that? Is that a shutter? He got me a shutter!" He clearly had a long, narrow item carefully tucked at his side. By that time, Bill met him on the down line with a slate. Charles wrote something on the slate, showed it to the camera, and waved to me. I was barely managing to choke back the tears when someone said, *"The lodge is intact!!"* I don't even remember who said it, but I was so overcome with emotion that I just wept uncontrollably.

Bill dives with the slate.

*Dave and I hear the incredible news
that Attakulla Lodge is intact!*
(Courtesy of WSPA - Spartanburg)

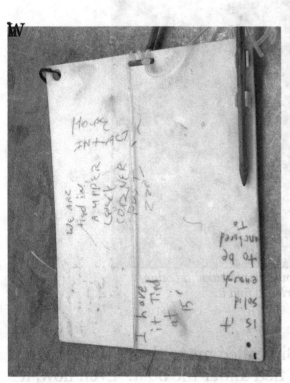

I finally see for myself: "House intact!"

When Jackie and Charles emerged from the water, their faces told me everything I had to know. Jackie later told me that 100 things *could* have gone wrong. 100 things. But none of them did. They both agreed it was one of the best dives they had ever been a part of. Not only did we confirm that the Lodge is intact, but a permanent down line was tied to a rear corner post, a post "solid enough to be anchored to." *Solid.* "I told you she was a tough ol' lady!" I exclaimed. Jackie talked about landing on a sloped roof, "like a sun porch." I knew immediately they had landed on the old kitchen at the back of the house. Charles described the horizontal windows that lined the wall of the dining hall. Just above these windows were smaller guest rooms where my

161

brother, 40 years earlier, had thrown an airplane out the window. It was from one of these rooms that Charles retrieved one of the most wonderful gifts I have ever received. Their 20 minutes of time on the bottom was running out, and he really wanted to bring something back to me. He saw this item sticking a little ways out the window, and he pulled, and pulled, and kept pulling, thinking to himself, "What is this thing?" It turned out to be one of the sidelights that used to stand on either side of the front door. The glass was gone, of course, but you could see where the wooden panes had once been in place. The bottom panel was partially broken, but the remaining wood still had warm brown paint on it, the sides still showing the remnants of white paint.

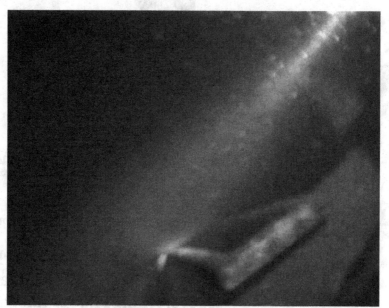

The sidelight rests on a window sill in Attakulla Lodge,
waiting for Charles to find it.

Once the divers removed their gear, Bill called me to the bow where they hoisted up the sidelight that had been tied under the boat. Even now, it's difficult for me to express the overwhelming joy I felt at that moment, not just for the gift of the sidelight, but to see the sheer excitement and sense of accomplishment on each person's face. It was time to celebrate our find. We made a great team!

Jackie

Charles

Bill

Back at the shop, we gathered around our treasure.
L-R: Bill Routh, Jackie Smith, Chris Salter, Charles Johnson, and me . . .

JOCASSEE JUNKIES!!!

"So, when's the next dive, guys?" I playfully chimed, barely giving them time to dry out from this one. They smiled.

And so we met again . . . the next weekend.

~

"Anyone know where there's a good underwater hotel around here?" I called from the parking lot, as I spotted Jackie and Charles. I was so glad to see them again. Our adventure the previous weekend definitely formed a bond between us, and I knew they were as anxious as I was about diving to the Lodge again. I offered to help tote equipment down to the boat and was unequivocally denied. "If you dive it, you carry it yourself," Bill advised. Well, at least I brought some snacks, which has now become my contribution to the team.

We made our way to the dive site. The guys were casually prepping their equipment when Kim said, "I hear something hissing." *Hissing* is not a good sound to hear around scuba tanks. We soon realized that the valve on one of Charles's tanks had gotten bumped on the trip, and it had been slowly leaking oxygen for 3 hours. We headed back to shore and waited as Bill and Charles went back to the shop for a refill. Back at the dive site, preparation began again – this time to discover a problem with an O-ring on one of the rebreathers and a flashlight that decided to malfunction. I was beginning to realize how many things could go wrong, as Jackie had cautioned me after the previous dive. Although time-consuming, however, the problems were easily fixed.

One of the goals of this dive was to confirm that the location of the down line was secure and that there would be no danger in anchoring directly to the Lodge's corner post. Bill found the underwater keg with the GPS locator and jumped in to retrieve the rope in order to anchor the boat. He was concerned about anchoring firmly to the Lodge, so he had attached a length of rope to the top of the keg. As Bill secured the line, Kim and Chris Salter, the safety divers, began to suit up. I was amused watching Kim

165

jump and wiggle into her stretchy suit. Ladies, we all know the difficulty getting into a new pair of panty hose; magnify that by 10, and that's what Kim was facing. She revealed to me one of her secrets for making it a little easier – *baby powder!* Charles was struggling to get one of his gloves on, and Kim offered some powder, which he dubiously accepted, not wanting to smell like a girl. The glove slipped on so easily that Charles commented, "Are you sure this thing is going to stay on?!"

Kim adjusts her suit.

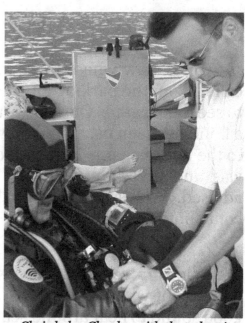

Chris helps Charles with that glove!

Kim is suited up.

Bill lends Chris a hand.

Chris is about ready.

The Salters offered Charles their new 650-foot depth-rated flashlight, since his was malfunctioning. He gratefully accepted, as lighting is definitely one thing you don't want to be without on a deep dive. Jackie and Charles hit the water, soon followed by Chris and Kim. Bill and I remained onboard, enjoying the pleasant day and light conversation.

A couple of hours later, they began to emerge, one by one. The one comment the divers consistently make is, "It's cold down there!" Grateful for sunshine and maybe a warm blanket, they told of their dive. Jackie and Charles were able to swim the entire perimeter of Attakulla Lodge, noting that overall she is quite sturdy. Some of the wood siding is loose, as nails have rusted, but her condition is very good. The extremely cold water with its low oxygen content and absence of light at the bottom has certainly contributed to her apparent lack of deterioration. "That front porch is huge!" Jackie commented. "I thought I'd never reach the end. The whole house is huge . . . it's just huge!" Charles was more intent in discussing his near disaster. The new flashlight he borrowed from Chris and Kim was apparently defective and *imploded* at 250 feet as he was quickly dropping on the down line, with no time to pull out his backup light. Alone in the pitch black, with 50 feet still to drop, he could barely see Jackie's pin spot of light. When they finally met, Charles showed Jackie the imploded light, and Jackie signaled *"UP?"* The thought crossed Charles's mind to call the dive due to this incident, but he felt very secure in continuing with such an experienced diver as Jackie. Charles has respectfully nicknamed Jackie *"The Heat"* – which means *the best*. Nevertheless, he said that the situation scared the life out of him, and it's a wonder he didn't have a heart attack. *"I almost s- - - in my drysuit!"* he exclaimed. Jackie replied, "You know, I heard a loud boom and thought to myself *'what are they doing up there?'"* I can't imagine the shot of adrenaline Charles experienced with a near sonic boom going off right in his hand! It was a great lesson in the importance of carrying redundant gear. We all laughed, and it further enforced the rumors of Charles's apparent frequent trouble with lights, the source of his nickname *"Light Destroyer."*

Charles wasn't the only one on this dive having trouble with lights, though. I couldn't believe that when I got back to my truck to come home, the battery was dead *because I left the lights on!* Jackie and Charles drove me to Bill's to look for some jumper cables. On the way I asked them: "So, is it really worth it to drive all this way, put on all that gear, and deal with the aggravation of equipment failures, all for just 20 minutes on the bottom?" Jackie looked at Charles in the rear-view mirror, and they both said, "Oh, *yeah!*" "It's not just the dive," Jackie said, "it's the camaraderie, all the preparation getting here, going down, and discussing the dive afterwards." I asked him what the Lodge looks like. He said, "She's beautiful. It's incredible as you drop down to see this huge house that looks like her roof is completely covered in snow." Charles said, "I wish I could just put you in a big bubble and take you down with me." So do I.

~

When Bill and I first discussed the possibility of locating Attakulla Lodge, he sent me an e-mail which said, "I would think that having it [a copy of the book] delivered by a diver to the porch of the Lodge would be fitting. Think about it." Boy, did I think about it . . . a lot! That seemed like such a pipe dream. It almost seemed too good to be true to even comprehend finding the Lodge, much less having a book dedication on the front porch. One thing I have learned about Bill Routh: he's a man of his word.

The day for the book dedication finally arrived – on September 4, 2004 – exactly a month to the day of Bill's discovery of the Lodge in the middle of the night. I asked Dot Jackson if she would do me the honor of attending. I have so admired her writings, and her encouragement was a big reason I published in the first place. Thankfully, she agreed to spend the day on the boat with me.

Dot Jackson and me,
enjoying the beauty
of the lake.

My heart was full of gratitude to so many people. I wanted to convey my love and appreciation to them by reading the following before the dive:

About 8 years ago, I started writing my memories of Jocassee for my girls to read one day. A few months later, I had the privilege of meeting Dot Jackson, a gifted author, who sat at the kitchen table reading my story and told me through her tears, "You have to publish this." In my wildest imagination, I never dreamed that would be possible, but Dot persisted in reminding me from time to time that I'd "better be writing that book!" So, Dot . . . this book is dedicated to you.

My husband Dave has supported me 110% in this entire project. I don't know how many nights he would come upstairs late at night while I worked at the computer and ask if I was ever coming to bed. He has patiently tolerated more Jocassee stories than any "northern boy" should ever have to hear. So, honey . . . this book is also dedicated to you.

My girls, Melissa and Pam, and my precious granddaughters, Miranda and Olivia, are my heartbeat. Girls . . . this book is also dedicated to you.

My Jocassee memories are all wrapped up in family, especially my mother Betty and brother Jimmy. This book is also dedicated to you.

To my heroes, Bill Routh, Charles Johnson, and Jackie Smith. Bill, since your first phone call to me a year and a half ago, you have not only dedicated your time and resources to finding Attakulla Lodge, but you have been there to encourage me when I heard continual rumors that the Lodge had floated off her foundation. Finding the Lodge intact would never have been possible without you. So, Bill . . . this book is also dedicated to you.

Jackie and Charles , you have literally put your life at risk to dive to a depth of 300 feet to confirm first-hand that Attakulla Lodge is indeed still standing. Your enthusiasm and support has meant the world to me, and the amazing gift you retrieved for me – the sidelight that used to stand beside the front door – is a rare treasure. One of my biggest regrets for the past 33 years has been that we never thought to take some token of remembrance from the Lodge – even just a door knob or a spindle from the bannister. My favorite Bible verse is Psalm 37:4: "Delight yourself in the Lord, and He will give you the desires of your heart." God used you that day to give me a desire of my heart. Charles and Jackie . . . this book is also dedicated to you.

Charles, I would consider it an honor if you would place a copy of my book on the front porch of Attakulla Lodge.

Reading the dedication to everyone.

Dave devised a method of protecting the book underwater. We put it between two pieces of plexiglass – like a sandwich – screwed it tightly together, and sealed all the edges with a thick layer of silicon. Charles attached a lanyard to the top, and we were good to go. Dave gathered everyone together for a group shot before sending the book down to the porch of the Lodge.

Just before the book's one-way trip to the bottom
Front L-R: Bill, Chris, Kim
Back L-R: Charles, Deb, Jackie

Just like "Where's Waldo?" Dave (top left) is always missing, because he's behind the camera. Here's the man behind all these wonderful pictures of the divers!

The divers suited up once again and jumped in. By now this seemed routine, but I guarantee you there is nothing routine about a 300-foot dive. I knelt down and handed Charles the book to deliver to the porch. What a thrill for me!

Jackie enters the water with a . . .

. . . big SPLASH!!

Charles is ready to deliver the book!

Bill prepares to hand the video camera to Jackie.

Charles displays the book encased in plexiglass.

173

Charles is underwater on the down line,
the book dangling on his arm. He and Jackie tossed a
coin to see who would place the book and who would
man the video camera.

As Jackie and Charles hit the bottom, Jackie was thrilled at the great video he was getting of the lake bottom, trees, and the Lodge. He was thinking to himself, "Oh, this is great! Debbie's gonna love this!" It was only when we viewed the video after the dive that we realized the camera had zoomed into macro mode, so nothing was discernable . . . except the one shot that we really wanted of Charles tying the book to the front porch.

As you can see, it's pitch black at the bottom. Look
carefully, and you can see the book as Charles places it on
the porch.

It's not easy swimming and filming at the same time. At first, it was presumed that Jackie had accidentally hit the zoom button on the camera. He was holding the camera by the lights on either side, however, and didn't touch any buttons at all – ever. The guys finally determined that the water pressure caused the camera to zoom in as they neared the bottom. Video up to that point was discernable. That didn't explain, though, why the camera suddenly focused in time to film Charles placing of the book, then mysteriously went out of focus very shortly thereafter. Jackie and Charles looked at each other, shrugged their shoulders, and Charles said, "Someone was looking out for us!" Truer words were never spoken. I give God the credit for this miracle.

Before this dive, Charles had told me that this would probably be his last dive here for a while. The demands of life were catching up, and he needed to take a breather. But when he surfaced, you could see the excitement on his face. "Well, I think I'll just rest for a few weeks . . . then go down again!" he smiled. He had just peeked in through the front door of the Lodge and can't wait to go in and look around. "She was calling to me, Deb . . . 'come in Charles, come in.' I gotta go back." Then he leaned in to me and whispered, "I touched her for you."

Charles was beaming when he surfaced!

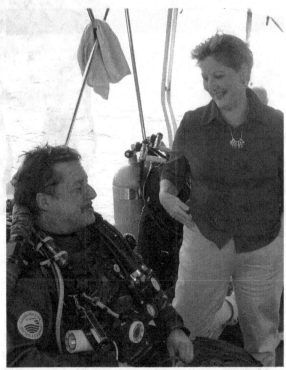

"She was calling to me to come in. I touched her for you."

Visibility – *vis*, as the divers call it – is the distance one can see underwater and has changed on each of these dives, varying from as little as 3 feet to 30 feet. No telling what causes it. It could be the draw from the intake turbines sucking upriver towards Bad Creek, or vice versa. Don't know. All I know is that each time they dive, Jocassee emotions flood my mind, stirred as easily as the silt on the bottom of the lake. A mere flick, and *poof!* they swirl around like a powdery cloud, taking its time to settle once again. I thought that locating Attakulla Lodge and placing my book on the front porch would signify the end of this chapter of my life. I'm just now beginning to see that it will never end, and I don't want it to. There is so much more to explore – so many questions yet to be answered. Attakulla Lodge is inviting us in . . .

This adventure is really just beginning.

Created by Mary Lou Cook

The following photographs were taken by my husband Dave Fletcher on the Jocassee dives previously documented. Please visit his website at
<u>www.FletcherImages.com</u>

Index of Pictures

Lake Jocassee:
What a Dive !!

Jocassee was pure, pristine,
And blue and green and crystal.
Of all things finite, it is . . .

Eternal.

Acknowledgments

I would like to express my sincere appreciation to the following people who have so generously given their time, information, and support to me while writing this book:

Dot Jackson and *Anna Simon* for encouraging me in the beginning to "write that book!"

Ron Rash for permission to quote from his poem "Deep Water"

Jane Yolen for permission to quote from "Letting Swift River Go"

Dennis Lawson, Corporate Archivist, Duke Power

Carlton Starnes, Real Estate Specialist, Duke Power

Jenny Howard for her Camp Jocassee brochure

My cousin *Claudia Whitmire Hembree* *
(for giving me the courage to go to the 30th floor!)

~

* Claudia Whitmire Hembree's book
Jocassee Valley
is available at www.jocasseevalley.com

Please visit my website at
www.JocasseeRemembered.com
for ordering information, news, video,
and more photos of the Jocassee Gorges

Sources

Cornelison, Fant, Hembree, and Robertson, *Journey Home*, The Greenville News-Piedmont Company, 1988

Hembree, Michael, and Jackson, Dot, *Keowee*, 1997

Rash, Ron, *Raising the Dead*, Iris Press, 2002

Yolen, Jane, *Letting Swift River Go*, Little Brown & Co., 1995

Duke Power Company archives

The Keowee Courier

The Independent Anderson

The Greenville News

Atlantic Mapping, Inc.

Printed in the United States
By Bookmasters